DEPART
FROM
EVIL

JOAN FIELDS LONG

Ordering Information:

Books to Life Marketing

KNOW YOUR BOOK'S PURPOSE TO LIFE

Books to Life Marketing Ltd
128 City Road, London, EC1V 2NX, UK

Printed in the United States of America

DEDICATION

To the members of the Christian Writer Group of Chapel Hill, N.C., many whom are now deceased for listening and for encouraging me when I was writing this book and reading it chapter by chapter at our meetings in 1977–78.

The original manuscript was typed on an electric typewriter by Annie Mae Price, now deceased. Thanks goes to Robert "Rabbit" Giles for typing it on the computer and to Larry Giles for helping send it to Author House Publishers. Also to my late husband, Cecil Long and to my children Allison Morris, Brent and Marcie Long and my grandchildren and for many friends for their encouragement to have it published. Most of all, I thank my Lord and Savior, Jesus Christ for giving me the ability to put words on paper.

CHAPTER 1

JENNY BENTLEY LOOKED up from the pair of blue denim overalls that she was patching for her husband Jed. She pushed back a wisp of red hair streaked with gray that had fallen across her forehead. With a sweaty hand, she touched her cheek that showed traces of faded freckles. It was hot. So hot that the overalls felt clammy as she held them up to inspect the patch on the knee.

"There," she said out loud. "That ought to last for at least one more wearin'."

She was sitting in a rocking chair on the wide front porch of the big old white framed house. It was the house in which Jed had been born. The bedroom they shared had been Jed's parents' room.

She got up and walked to the edge of the porch. A big yellow cat came up the steps and began to wind himself around her bare legs.

"Quincy, stop that touchin' me. It's too hot to have you rubbin' all over me. You lazy good for nothin' cat, get out yonder to the barn and catch those mice that keep cuttin' our feed bags. I'll find myself patchin' them like I've been patchin' Jed's overalls."

As if he understood her every word, the cat slowly went down the steps, stretching his long body, and wandered lazily around the corner of the house.

Jenny looked across the grassy front yard toward the dirt road that ran in front of the house. She could see a cloud of dust in the distance.

"Must be the mailman," she thought. "He's late today. I do hope we'll get a letter from Jason. That boy hasn't written since he went to South America."

Jenny started down the steps toward the mailbox at the side of the road. She realized that the approaching automobile was not Mr. Weathers, the mailman. It was a blue car pulling a U-Haul-It trailer. The car turned in the driveway and came to a halt. Jenny could see that it was occupied by two people, or was it three? The driver stopped the noisy engine and stepped from the car. A short heavy set man in a dingy white shirt and floppy brown necktie walked toward Jenny. He was smiling and Jenny sensed there was nothing to be alarmed about.

"Hello," the stranger said in a cheerful voice. "Is this the Jed Bentley place?"

"Yes," answered Jenny.

The man stuck out his right hand. "You must be Mrs. Bentley. I'm Thomas Wilson and this is my wife Cybele," indicating toward the car. "I'm the new pastor at your church."

"Mr. Wilson," Jenny replied, pumping his hand. "How nice to meet you. Get out Mrs. Wilson and come on in out of this heat."

The car door opened with a loud squawk as if it had been a long time without oil. The paint on the car was faded and scratched. The left back fender was dented and the side that Jenny saw was caked with dried mud. Mrs. Wilson stepped out and stretched her long arms high above her head. She was tall and slim. Long blond straight hair, parted in the middle fell around her shoulders and clung to the blue shirt that she was wearing. It was as faded as the blue jeans that dragged the ground around her bare feet.

A large black dog bounded over the front seat and dashed into the yard. It ran between Jenny and Mr. Wilson.

Jenny thought she had never seen such a big dog in all her life!

"Czar, get back in the car," Mr. Wilson commanded. "Cybele, keep the door open so he can get back in."

The dog did not obey. He spied Quincy, the cat, and took off after him. He began to bark with a loud throaty sound that made Jenny shiver.

"Mr. Wilson, is your dog friendly?" she stammered.

"You don't have a thing to worry about. This is one Doberman Pincher that is as friendly as can be."

"You all come on in," Jenny said. "I suppose when he gets done chasin' our cat, he'll come back."

In the meantime, Quincy had run up the nearest oak tree and was sitting on a limb looking down at the noisy creature below.

The dog jumped onto the far end of the porch. As Jenny held the door open, he squeezed in front of Mrs. Wilson and ran into the house. Both Mr. and Mrs. Wilson went in after him, shouting his name and telling him to come back. He ran down the hall, through the dining room and into the kitchen. With a loud crash, he knocked the back door screen open. Master and mistress followed the same trail.

Jenny went to the kitchen and watched from the doorway as they pursued the fast moving black object all over the backyard.

Finally, the dog lay down flat on his belly, paws out front with his head resting on them as if he was ashamed of his performance.

"Cybele, go get his chain," Mr. Wilson said. "I'll hold him here. Czar, you aren't behaving very well. I guess you are tired of riding. You need to stretch your legs. Mrs. Bentley, do you mind if I tie him to your clothes line? That way he can get some exercise without disturbing anything."

"That will be fine, Mr. Wilson." Jenny thought that she was glad she had done her Monday morning wash early and had it back in the house.

Mrs. Wilson returned with the chain and with much urging they were able to tie the reluctant Czar to the clothes line.

"Mrs. Bentley, may I have a pan of water for him?" Mr. Wilson asked.

"Certainly," Jenny replied. "Look there at the well house and you'll find a pan. Fill it at the spigot. And you two come in and I'll fix you a glass of ice tea. I know you are about to perish after that chase."

Jenny went to the refrigerator, filled three glasses with ice and poured in sparkling tea from a pitcher. Ice tea could always be found in Jenny's refrigerator in the summer. She made a fresh gallon every morning.

The three of them sat down at Jenny's yellow topped dinette table.

"Well, let me have a look at you two," Jenny said. "Things have been happenin' so fast since you arrived, I really haven't seen you."

What Jenny saw was two people that looked as if they did not belong together. Mrs. Wilson was very pretty in a plain sort of way.

Her long straight blond hair framed an oval shaped face. Her eyes were light blue with blond lashes. Fair skin held no sign of makeup and her lips, though pink, were their natural color. A wide mouth showed even white teeth when she smiled. Mr. Wilson was short and rather on the stocky side. Dark hair showing flecks of gray was very thin on the top of his head. Long sideburns grew down the ruddy sunburned face. His eyes were deep blue with thick dark brows.

Jenny spoke, "We were not expectin' you until next week. I'm afraid you'll find your house is a mess. Some of the ladies from the church and I planned to clean it later in the week. It has been some time since anyone lived there. Mr. and Mrs. Jones moved in April. Or I should say Mr. Jones moved. Poor old Mrs. Jones took sick and in four months she went to be with the Lord. Bless her heart, she had cancer."

"Mr. Jones was your former pastor?" Mr. Wilson asked.

"That's right, and a good one too," Jenny replied. "His health was failin', so he decided to go to Florida to live with one of their daughters. The house is all furnished, except for linens and dishes and of course groceries. Did you ride past it on your way here?"

"No," replied Mr. Wilson. "We stopped in Langdon and asked how to find your place. Your husband said in one of his letters that he kept the key to the parsonage and the church at your house."

"Yes," Jenny answered. Before she could say any more, a big man dressed in blue overalls and a checked shirt stepped through the kitchen door. Jed Bentley stood six feet four in his stocking feet and weighed at least 235 pounds. Beads of sweat stood on his sunburned face and trickled into the corners of his dark twinkling eyes.

Mr. Wilson stood up as Jed came in. They shook hands, exchanging names before Jenny could introduce them. Cybele quietly remained seated, but held out a dainty hand for Jed to squeeze in his big rough one.

"Let me get you same tea, honey," Jenny drawled.

"Thanks, I sure could use some. It is awfully hot for June. Wonder what July will be like," Jed said, wiping his forehead with a red-bandana handkerchief. He sat down with the others around the table.

"Welcome to our home and community," Jed continued.

"Thank you," Mr. Wilson replied, smiling.

"That your dog tied to our clothesline?" Jed asked.

"Sure is," said Mr. Wilson. "I'm afraid he made a grand entrance into your home, and I must apologize for it. He ran through the house as if he owned it. Do you have a dog?"

"Yes, our Lady has been with us for seven years. Raised her from a pup. She is a full blooded collie and helps keep our cows in line. You know, I can trust that dog to drive all thirty-six cows from one pasture to another," Jed said with a faint brag in his voice.

"Thirty-six cows!" Mr. Wilson exclaimed, licking his lips. "That's a lot of steak!"

"They aren't beef cattle," Jed answered. "They are dairy cows."

"Anyway, that's a lot of milk and butter," laughed Mr. Wilson. "How do you manage all this, you must have some help?"

"Sure do," said Jed. "Ike Wade and his two sons are my main help. Ike lives in our tenant house. They are waitin' for me down in the south pasture. I came up here to get some staples and a new roll of wire. We have a fence down near the creek that needs repairin'. Come on and go with me and you can meet them and see a little of this land. But first, get shut of that necktie! Jenny, have you got some of that ice tea that you can send Ike and the boys?"

Jenny hurried to fix the tea. Mr. Wilson took off his tie and tossed it to Cybele.

"I'm going to call you Jed, and please call me Thomas. And that goes for you too, Jenny. No more of this Mr. Wilson. See you later, hon," Thomas called over his shoulder as the two men went out the door.

CHAPTER 2

IKE WADE LEANED on the post hole diggers he was using. He removed his dirty cap from his sweaty head. He wiped his brown face with the sleeve of his shirt.

"This ground sure is hard," he commented.

"Don't know why this fence had to be fixed today. It's too hot to work," Sam Wade said lazily. He rolled from his back to his stomach in the cool green grass of the pasture. He had removed his shirt and the muscles in his chocolate colored arms and back glistened with beads of perspiration.

"You can say that while you loll around," Ike answered, lifting more dirt. "You don't even know what a day's work is."

"I'll never find out, if I can help it," Sam laughed. "Playing football is hard enough work."

"Don't let football go to your head, boy," his father answered. "You'd better get an education and maybe you won't have to work as hard as me and my pappy has."

Sam got up and lifted a new creosote coated post into the hole his father had finished. "All your work for Jed Bentley hasn't got you anywhere."

"You watch what you say. There isn't no better friend to me on this earth than Jed," Ike replied. "We grew up together. We used to swim and fish in that very creek." He pointed toward the creek that lazily made its way between banks lined with dark green bushes.

"Yeah" Sam retorted. "I've heard you tell all those tales before. I guess when I get older I'll recall all those times that Jason Bentley and I had fights. That sissy thinks he can play football, but he wasn't a drop in the bucket at Langdon High School compared to me. I'm glad that he was two years ahead of me. I really would have hated makin' him look bad." He laughed loudly.

Ike sat down on the grass, stretching his long legs. "I just never will understand you guys."

"Not much to understand." Sam replied. He took out a comb from his pocket and began picking his afro-hair-do that was getting limp from the heat. "I just plain do not like the Bentleys. That stuck up JoAnna makes me want to puke. I asked her to dance with me at our graduation ball. She turned me down flat. Man, those other girls thought it a pleasure to dance with the star football player."

"Sam, you have no cause to dislike the Bentleys. They've been good to us. They furnish the house we live in. They pay our salary and we're treated fair and square by them. You've eat a many a T-bone steak from the beef that Jed butchers and gives us every year. And whose land do the vegetables grow on that you put in your belly?"

"I still don't have to like them," Sam replied.

Junie Wade came up from the creek where he had been wading. He was three years younger than Sam. He was tall like Sam, but somewhat thinner.

"Still, I don't understand you either," Junie said, sitting down to put on his worn tennis shoes. "JoAnna never has treated me wrong. She and I have long talks about school and her horse."

"That's because you are younger than she is, little brother," Sam replied. "Come August and I'll be long gone from this place. If I had my way, I'd have gone to New York to stay with Uncle James and worked this summer. But no, you had to go and promise Jed Bentley that I'd stay here and work in this milk factory."

"You'd better be glad that you are here where you got some clean air to breath," his father said. "All that stuff that your Uncle James brags about ain't so. You think he owns that Cadillac he was drivin' the last time he came down here. Well, his new wife that he brought along told your mother that it was her car and she only lets him drive it." Ike let out a long laugh that echoed through the green pasture.

Junie spoke seriously, "Dad I been aimin' to bring somethin' up to you. It's about Aunt Tempie."

"What you talkin' about son?" his father asked.

"Well, last night after everybody was in bed, I wasn't sleepy, so I was lookin' out the window. The moon was shinin' and I saw somebody walkin' toward the old spring house. I was about to come in and wake you up, when I saw that it was Aunt Tempie."

"Where was she goin' at that time of night? She knows we have indoor plumbin'." Sam snickered.

"I don't know," answered Junie. "I watched a while longer and she came back and went into her room. I've seen her go out at night before."

"You and Mama are goin' to have to put that old crazy woman in an insane asylum," Sam declared. "I've known she was peculiar for a long time. Kids at school tease me about havin' a witch for an aunt. One of my dates one night asked me if my aunt made me any love potions.

I told her I didn't need any potions to make me know how to love!"

Ike scratched his head. "She always has made up herb medicines and give them to folks. I ain't never thought of her as no witch. Witches are mean and Aunt Tempie ain't got a mean bone in her old skinny body."

"Next time I see her go out at night, I'm goin' to follow her," Junie said.

"Better not Junie-boy, she might cast a spell on you and you'd turn into a frog," Sam teased.

"Hush such talk!" Ike said. "Here comes Jed with the wire. Looks like he's got somebody with him."

Jed introduced Mr. Wilson to the three Wades. He gave them the ice tea.

"Mighty nice of Miss Jenny," Ike said drinking his tea. "So you are the new preacher Jed's been telling us was comin' in."

"Jed tells me that you are a Christian," Mr. Wilson addressed Ike.

"That's right, sir." He rolled his big brown eyes. "I have loved and served the Lord for nigh onto twenty-five years," Ike replied humbly. "My pappy was a preacher and he wanted me to be one. The nearest I've got is bein' a deacon in my church."

"All do not receive the same spiritual gifts," Mr. Wilson said. Looking at Sam, "I hear you are a football player and have a scholarship."

"Yeah. I'll be going to the University in August. Junie is a good player, too."

"I like basketball better," Junie replied shyly.

"All this fresh air and sunshine is good for everybody," Mr. Wilson said. He breathed deeply and looked around him. "Where I've been living is full of smog."

"Would that have been California?" Sam asked.

"Yes, and I'm glad to be away from there."

"I've always wanted to go to California," Sam said dreamily.

"Perhaps you will one day," Mr. Wilson replied.

"One thing for certain, I'm not goin' tospend the rest of my life in this God forsaken place." Sam retorted.

Mr. Wilson hesitated a moment before speaking. "Sam, why do you call this place God forsaken? Look all around you—everywhere—you see God's creation. These rolling green hills, the willows along the creek, the tall majestic pine trees in the distance-no indeed this place isn't God forsaken! Remember the Psalm, 'I will lift up mine eyes unto the hills, from whence cometh my help. My help cometh from the Lord, which made heaven and earth.'"

"No sermons, please Preacher. I get enough of that from my Dad I just can't see spendin' all my life on a dairy farm. Especially one that belongs to somebody else." He jammed the post hole digger into the hard earth and came up with a scoop of red clay.

"What about you?" Mr. Wilson addressed Junie. "Do you share your brother's feelings?'"

"No, sir. I want to be a veterinarian and practice right here in my own county. I love animals."

"Mr. Wilson, that boy really has a way with animals." Ike spoke.

"He always has been able to tame the wildest creatures. Even these milk cows will mind him. Junie can even get along with that old mean bull that Jed keeps."

"Bull, what bull? Where is he?" Mr. Wilson asked excitedly.

Jed laughed, "Don't worry he's tied up near the barn. The pen is good and strong. You must feel about bulls the way I do about your Doberman Pincher."

"You have a Doberman?" Junie asked.

"Sure do. Gentlest dog I ever owned. I figure dogs are a lot like people. Love them enough and you'llbe able to see the best instead of always the worst in them."

"I know some dogs that I like better than some people," Sam laughed as he helped stretch the wire between the new posts.

Jed drove the last staple. The men gathered up the tools and climbed into the truck.

"Time to go milk those cows," Jed said looking toward the west where the sun was beginning to drop behind the pine trees.

CHAPTER 3

JENNY BENTLEY'S KITCHEN was her own private sanctuary. It's yellow walls, shiny white cabinets and waxed vinyl tile floor reflected the real Jenny. The Jenny that took pride in making her house a home for those she loved. Even the curtains were starched and ironed free of every wrinkle. Each appliance had been carefully selected by its owner and cared for with loving hands.

Cybele Wilson looked around Jenny's kitchen. She thought of a place far away. A place where she had not been for many years. She remembered the smells and the sounds of her own mother's kitchen. An image of her mother standing at the double sinks washing and rinsing dishes came before her eyes. Suddenly she got up from her chair and walked toward the sink with her arm out as if she were going to embrace someone. Realizing there was no one standing there, she picked up a glass from the counter and filled it with water. She gulped the water hoping Jenny had not noticed her action.

Jenny was talking and did not see Cybele's dream like movements. She was telling Cybele about their lives. About Jason in South America with Vista volunteers and how much she missed him. And about Joanna being away for two weeks as a counselor at a Bible camp and how much her horse missed her.

"Wouldn't you like to go over and see where you all will be livin'?" Jenny asked.

"Sure", Cybele replied. "Could we take Czar along so he can get used to his new home?"

Apprehensive Jenny swallowed hard, hoping Cybele wouldn't notice, and replied, "All right. Seems he's settled down. I'll get the VW bus out of the garage while you get him." Certainly hope she keeps him on the leash Jenny thought.

Jenny backed the blue and white bus out of the garage and Cybele and the big dog hopped in. The dog sat on the middle seat and panted his hot breath on the back of Jenny's neck.

"I must not be afraid of him" Jenny said out loud.

"No need to be," replied Cybele. "He is very gentle and loves everyone. I gave him to my husband as a wedding present."

"How long you been married?" Jenny asked as she guided the VW onto the main road from her driveway.

"Six months."

"You're still a bride. Just wait until you've been married 25 years. They have been happy years. Jed's a good husband. He's kind and considerate. We've had our disputes of course, but nothin' ever serious. In fact, I'd say the Lord has been very good to us."

"Have you always lived here?" Cybele asked as she gazed out the window and watched the rolling green hills passing by.

"All my life. I was born about three miles from where we live now. Jed and I went to the same school and same church. There it is now, the church I mean. Your house is just beyond".

Jenny slowed down and Cybele exclaimed, "It's lovely! I'd like to do an oil painting. It's so shiny white and clean looking and the steeple is so—so right."

"You're an artist. I just knew you were when I met you," Jenny said. "Out back of the church is the graveyard. That's where my parents and Jed's are buried. Also, our first baby. Let's take a look at your new home first."

Jenny stopped the VW in the driveway of the white framed parsonage. "It isn't the grandest place in the world, but it is comfortable."

As they got out of the car, Czar jumped out and began running around the house. He arrived on the front porch just as Jenny unlocked the door. He bounded into the living room. He ran to each piece of furniture sniffing as if he was looking for something. Then into the front bedroom he ran and leaped onto the bed. He stretched out his long body with his head on his paws and looked as if he was announcing that he had found his place.

Jenny screamed at him before she realized what she was doing. "Get off that bed, Czar!"

Cybele walked past the bedroom door as if she didn't see the dog and continued to open doors and inspect the rooms and closets.

"Czar," Jenny pleaded. "That was the bed Mrs. Jones died in. Would you please get off it before you make it smell like a dog and get hairs all over it." She reached for his collar to pull him off. A low growl came from his throat and Jenny ran into the hall calling Cybele.

"He snapped at me!"

Cybele answered calmly, "You must be mistaken. Czar never Has bitten anyone." She went into the bedroom. "Czar, get off the bed." He did not move.

She reached for his collar and gently but firmly pulled him from the bed. No sooner had she turned his collar loose, when he jumped back into the middle of the bed. Cybele ignored his disobedience and went into the kitchen.

"Nice kitchen. Guess I'll have to learn to cook."

"You don't know how to cook?" Jenny asked.

"Not much. Where we've been living since we were married I wasn't responsible for meals."

"Well, I'll teach you," Jenny assured her. "Nothin' I like better than cookin'. This place isn't as dirty as I'd thought. A little dustin' and you'll be able to move in. You all can sleep at our house tonight. This is Wednesday and we'll have prayer meetin'. We'd better be gettin' home and fixin' some dinner for those hungry men."

"Could we stop in and see the church?" Cybele asked.

"Yes, we'll walk over and take a look."

Cybele seemed unable to take her eyes off the white structure. She stood in one spot and gazed as the evening sun cast shadows across the grassy lawn.

"This is where I'll set my easel. Let's go inside."

Jenny unlocked the door.

"It's so quaint and beautiful!" Cybele exclaimed. "God must surely be in this place." She walked slowly down the red carpeted aisle touching each shiny wooden pew with her right hand. "I'll paint a picture of the inside, too."

Jenny waited patiently in the vestibule. It was cool inside the closed building even though it was not air-conditioned.

Cybele returned. "Guess you think I'm crazy carrying on like this over a building!"

"No. We like this building too. It holds such fond memories for all of us. I'm sure you and your husband will receive many blessin's and great joy pastorin' here. You' ll find the congregation very cooperative. Most folks here are just like Jed and me, born and raised in this community and church."

They walked back to the VW.

"Wonder what has happened to Czar," Cybele said.

"I forgot all about him," answered Jenny "Did we lock him up in the parsonage? We'd better take a look."

She unlocked the front door and both women called the dog by name. They went from room to room looking under furniture and into closets, but no Czar.

Cybele ran out back calling him.

Jenny locked the door again and walked toward the church. Cybele joined her and they went toward the graveyard calling him.

Cybele saw him first. She pointed. "There he is beyond that tombstone."

Jenny exclaimed. "Why that's Mrs. Jones' grave!"

Czar was digging with his big paws and sniffing into the ground and making throaty noises.

"Stop that, Czar!" Cybele shouted.

"My goodness!" the distraught Jenny said out loud. "He is tearin' up poor Mrs. Jones' grave. And Mr. Jones had it fixed all smooth with white sand."

Cybele tried to grab him by the collar, but he jerked away each time and kept digging and sniffing.

Both women were shouting at him and pleading with him to follow them to the car. Suddenly he stopped digging. Stood up on all four legs with his head held high in the air. His pointed ears were laid back as if he heard a distant call. He took off running and disappeared around the corner of the church with the women in hot pursuit.

Jenny slowed down to catch her breath and spoke angrily, "That's the dumbest dog I've ever seen in my life."

Cybele stopped running. "He really isn't dumb, just independent. Let's go back to your house. Perhaps we'll see him on the way."

They got into the VW and Jenny drove slowly so they could look on both sides of the road for a moving black object.

"I dread telling Tom that Czar is missing." Cybele sighed.

"Oh! He'll come back," Jenny replied. "We had an old hound dog once that stayed gone for two weeks. One mornin' I got up and there he was standin' on my back door steps beggin' for food."

They arrived at Jenny's.

"I'll not put the VW in the garage as we'll be drivin' it to prayer meetin' tonight. From the looks of the sun it's milkin' time. I'd better hurry up and set the table and warm up supper before I go out to the milk house to check on things there."

"Do you help with the milking?" Cybele asked.

"Not too much anymore—as long as Jed has plenty of help. It's much easier than it used to be. We have pipes runnin' from the milkers in the barn into a tank in the milk house and actually the milk is never touched by our hands. It is all done by electricity. Things have really changed since we took over this farm after Jed got out of the Army. He was in the Korean War. We got married when he came home on leave after his basic trainin'." Jenny chattered away as she prepared their meal.

"Want to go with me to the barn and see the cows. Your husband must be out there with Jed."

They started walking toward the big red barn.

Cybele let out a happy yell. "Look, there's Czar! He's lying under the clothesline." She quickly fastened the chain attached to the clothesline to his collar. Reaching down she gave him a loving pat on his black shiny head. "You naughty dog, you had me scared. I thought you had run away."

Jenny shivered as she walked past him.

CHAPTER 4

THE COWS WERE milked and turned into the pasture near the barn for the night. JoAnna's horse, Duke, was fed and watered. The old mule, "Miz Maud" was munching corn and the bull had been tended.

Ike and his sons went to their home and the Bentley's and their guests sat down to what Jenny called a regular Monday night supper. The meal was blessed by one of Jed's long prayers that included giving thanks for all the Lord had provided including the care and safety of JoAnna and Jason.

Thomas Wilson ate and complimented Jenny with every bite.

Cybele picked at her food.

Jenny tried not to notice. After a while she could not contain her thoughts. "Cybele, you aren't eatin' anythin."

Cybele replied, "I'm sorry, I'm just not a big eater. Thomas makes up for me." She laughed nervously.

Thomas smiled and continued to eat. "I guess Cybele forgot to tell you, she's a vegetarian. Good thing too with the price of meat these days. I like all foods and especially good cooking like this Mrs. Bentley."

"A vegetarian," Jenny pondered. "Well, you'll have plenty to eat around here. Everyone has a garden. In fact the string beans and squash came out of ours. Some of the first for this summer. Later in the week I'll be canning beans."

"Cybele, Mrs. Bentley will have to give you lessons in canning and freezing," Thomas smiled lovingly at his pretty wife.

17

"And she'll have to give me art lessons," Jenny replied. "Jed, Cybele is an artist. She plans to paint a picture of our church."

Jed answered between bites of apple pie and ice cream that Jenny had just served. "Mrs. Wilson, you couldn't have a better cookin' instructor than my Jenny. I don't know how well she would do in art lessons. There's a lot of beauty in this part of the country to capture on a canvas. Used to do a little sketching when I was a boy."

"We'd better hurry along if we aim to get to prayer meetin' on time," Jenny said.

Cybele looked at Thomas and in a shy voice asked, "May I be excused from going this evening? I'm very tired. I'd like to go to bed early."

Thomas did not answer right away. "That's your decision. I'm anxious to meet the people of our new church." He excused himself from the table and went upstairs to the room that Jenny had assigned them.

Cybele helped Jenny remove the dishes from the table. Jenny quickly placed them in the dishwasher.

"I would stay here and keep you company, but it's my night to keep the nursery," Jenny said as she folded the checkered apron she had been wearing.

"That's okay. I really do want to go to bed early. Jenny, is there some place I could go shopping before Sunday. To tell the truth, these are the only clothes I have."

"I'd be happy to take you shoppin'. Langdon has quite a few stores. Or we could go to Rockville. They have a nice new mall."

Jenny, Jed and Thomas went to the church. Jed proudly introduced Thomas as the new pastor they had all been waiting for the Lord to send.

The hour passed quickly with songs, prayers and a short Bible study. After the meeting, Thomas shook hands with the entire congregation.

They closed the building and Jenny and Jed showed Thomas the parsonage. He was very pleased withhis new home. They drove the short distance back home with Thomas talking all the way about the warm reception he had received.

When they opened the front door they heard a loud bark from upstairs.

Thomas looked at Jenny and Jed. "Sounds like Cybele has company," he said.

Cybele and Czar came down the steps. She was restraining him by the collar. Realizing she needed to give an explanation to the three people gazing up at her, she said, "Czar ran away again. He got loose from his chain. Sam and Junie brought him to the front door. They said he was in their yard barking at their Aunt Tempie.

"How did they ever get him to come here?" Jenny asked—remembering the experience of the afternoon.

"The younger one, he has a real charm with animals. Some how he coaxed Czar into following him", Cybele replied.

"I'll shut him up in our car," Thomas said. "Come along you naughty dog, Mrs. Bentley doesn't want you in her nice clean house."

Jenny whispered an amen.

Cybele went back up the stairs without saying a word.

Thomas came back in. "He'll settle down for the night. He is used to sleeping in the car."

Jenny asked if she could get him anything.

"Is there any more of that delicious apple pie?"

"There is a piece just for you," Jenny replied as she went into the kitchen.

Jed and Thomas sat down in the den. This room, like the kitchen was warm and inviting. The brightly flowered pillows on the brown leather couch matched the drapes. Both had been made by Jenny.

The conversation turned again to the church. Thomas asked Jed and Jenny many questions as he ate his pie. Jenny allowed Jed to answer most of his questions. Even though she enjoyed talking, she respected her husband as being her head as Christ is the head of the church.

The antique clock on the mantle struck 10:00. Jed yawned and said, "Preacher, as much as I am enjoyin' this conversation, those old cows will be expectin' to be milked mighty early in the mornin'.

Thomas excused himself and went upstairs.

Jenny and Jed went into their bedroom. Once in bed, Jenny could contain herself no longer.

"Well, what do you think of them?

Jed chuckled as he answered. "I knew you were dying to ask. Seem like fine folks to me. Maybe a little different from what we're used to, but give them a little time and they'll be one of us."

"That dog is what gets me," Jenny declared. "This afternoon he was out in the graveyard diggin' as hard as he could in Mrs. Jones' grave. And no amount of scoldin' could make him stop".

"Probably after a mole that was under the ground." Jed yawned.

"I just don't know," Jenny replied. "Cybele doesn't seem to be able to control him. She is a different sort than I had expected for a pastor's wife."

"Now, Jenny, let's don't go classin' preacher's wives as any different from anyone else".

"Good night, honey. I love you," Jed said sleepily.

"Good night, darlin'—I love you, too."

Jenny didn't fall asleep right away. She went over in her mind the events of the day. She prayed silently for Thomas and Cybele. She prayed for herself that she would be able to tolerate the dog. Just before she fell asleep she asked the Lord's blessing on JoAnna and Jason.

Jenny and Jed both sat up in bed as a bright flash of lightning split the sky. The thunder rumbled loudly.

"We're really havin' a storm", Jed said yawning sleepily.

Jenny got up and closed the East window where rain was beginning to blow in on her white sheer curtains

"Listen, Jed", she said excitedly.

"What you want me to listen to? All I hear is thunder and lightnin'".

"Listen, I hear the cows bawlin'. I hear Duke. And that dog is barkin'! I wonder if he is out of the car and botherin' the animals."

Jed got up and stood beside her at the window.

"Hm, guess that storm has excited the cows. Sort of unusual though, they don't usually carry on because of a little thunder storm. I think I hear a dog barkin' and it isn't Lady."

"Jed, I have a feelin' that our new pastor's dog is more than we bargained for when we hired him. Maybe he'll get run over by a truck," Jenny said as she climbed back into bed.

"Seems the storm is subsidin'," Jed said. He slipped back into bed. "Don't think there is any need to go out to the barn. They'll settle down on their own."

"If that dog would stop barkin'," Jenny added.

They heard footsteps on the stairs and the front door opening. Thomas spoke to the dog in a commanding voice, "Quieten down! Hush your barking!" The dog stopped barking and in a few minutes Jenny and Jed heard the front door close again.

CHAPTER 5

AFTER A HUGE breakfast of sausage, pancakes and eggs, Thomas Wilson pushed his chair back from the table and said, "Mrs, Bentley, I don't know which I enjoyed more, your dinner last night or this breakfast."

Jenny, glowing in the compliment, replied, "Glad you enjoyed it. Sorry that Cybele didn't feel like comin' down for breakfast."

"She never eats breakfast. In fact she eats very little. Cost me more to feed Czar than it does her," Thomas laughed. "Guess we'd better pull the trailer on over to our new house and unload."

The Wilsons left and Jenny went about her housework.

Jed came to the house after milking the cows and had a second cup of coffee. That was one of the things Jenny liked about her husband's occupation. As a dairy farmer, he was never very far away and was always coming to the house for a cup of coffee or a glass of iced tea.

Thomas and Cybele arrived at their new home. Thomas unlocked the door. "Cybele, this is our first real house and I'm going to carry you over the threshold." He scooped the slender figure up into his arms and carried her into the living room. "And now, Mrs. Wilson you are officially the keeper of this home, the one I love most in this world.

This is a new beginning for both of us." He kissed her before dropping her onto the couch. As they came in the door, Czar squeezed his long sleek body beside them and reached the couch at the same time as Cybele. All three fell into a heap on the couch. Cybele was carrying a large denim bag. Upon impact, the bag fell open. Its contents spilled on the floor.

Thomas stood up as he saw what came out of the bag. His voice was unsteady as he tried to suppress his anger. "Cybele, I thought I told you to get rid of that stuff. Why did you bring that old ouija board, and those tarot cards and even horoscope charts?" He kicked the board across the floor.

Cybele spoke in a timid voice, "I really meant to throw them away. But my Aunt Phoebe gave them to me. They belonged to my grandmother. I just had to keep them".

Thomas came and sat down beside her. Putting his arm around her sagging shoulder, he spoke more calmly, "I'm sorry honey, I shouldn't shout at you. I must remember there are a lot of things that I know and believe that you've never even heard. These things (pointing to the contents of the bag) represent things of the devil. As a Christian, I deplore anything that is evil. Cybele, you may not realize this, but Satan has his demons in this world. They work through things of the occult."

Cybele didn't answer. She quickly gathered the things up and ran into the front bedroom.

"Cybele, I'll unload the trailer now. We need to turn it in at a service station in town and pick up a few groceries. Have to be only a few. Our funds are very low. We've used up almost all the travel advance the church sent us. Wonder when it'll be payday."

They unloaded the trailer which consisted mainly of Thomas' books that he had collected over the years. A few clothes, a battered stereo set, about two dozen records, an ancient typewriter, and an easel and a few paintings were soon put in the house that was already furnished with bare necessities.

The trip to Langdon took a short time. By lunch they were back and the groceries stored away. Thomas helped himself to a bologna sandwich while Cybele munched on celery and carrots. Czar contentedly chewed on a bone that a kind butcher in one of the stores sent him when he found that Thomas was the new pastor.

"Think I'll take a nap," Thomas yawned. "This humidity is getting me down. I'll work on my sermon for Sunday when I wake up."

"I'll take a walk. I like the outdoors. Aren't the trees around here beautiful? And have you ever seen such green pastureland and all the wild flowers. I know I'm goin' to like it here," Cybele said.

"Don't get lost, darling," Thomas said as he kissed her forehead. "And watch out for snakes."

"Oh! I'm not afraid of snakes. They rather fascinate me. I'll take Czar along. He won't let me get lost."

On Friday morning, Jenny called Cybele to see if she would like to go shopping. Cybele said she'd be ready when Jenny came by for her.

They drove to Langdon and looked at dresses for Cybele. She didn't find one she liked. Jenny suggested they go to the new mall at Rockville.

They walked into the cool mall with it's windows decorated with the latest fashion. Someone called Jenny's name.

"Vera Gray, when did you get back from Europe?" Jenny drawled.

"Jenny, it's so good to see you." The two women embraced.

"Vera, you look stunnin' as usual."

It was true. Vera Gray looked like one of the store window models. Her dyed blonde hair was exquisitely done. Her makeup was perfect. She was wearing a light green polyester suit with shoes and purse to match.

"Let me introduce you to the wife of our new pastor," Jenny said. "Vera Gray, I'd like to present Cybele Wilson. They arrived from California on Wednesday. They are all settled down in the parsonage.

"So nice to meet you," Vera said enthusiastically. "Guess a lot of interesting things have been going on since I've been away."

"Glad to meet you," Cybele said shyly. "While the two of you catch up, I'll go in this little dress shop and see what I can find. Excuse me, please."

Jenny and Vera moved away from the center walkway of the mall.

"So that's the pastor's wife," Vera said, raising her penciled eyebrows above her green-rimmed sunglasses. "Does she always wear faded shirts and jeans?!

Jenny smiled, "So far that's all I've seen her wear. She is here to buy a dress and shoes. Evidently her wardrobe is very limited." "What's Mr. Wilson like?" Vera asked.

"Well," Jenny drawled, "He's a mite older than Cybele. He's not very tall and a little on the heavy side. You'll get to hear him preach on Sunday."

"How's Jed?"

"Fine, busy as ever."

"What's happening with Jason and Joanna.?"

"Jason is in South America with a group of Vista Volunteers workin' on an agricultural project. Haven't heard from him other than a postcard sayin' he arrived safely. Joanna has been gone for two weeks as a counselor at Bible camp. She'll be home tomorrow. It will be so good to have her here again."

Vera looked at her watch. "I must run. I have an appointment with my lawyer at 1:00. Be seeing you on Sunday at church. Bye-now."

"Good-bye Vera. Nice seein' you." Jenny looked around for Cybele. Cybele came walking swiftly toward Jenny.

"Ready to go," Cybele said.

"You mean you found a dress?" Jenny asked.

Cybele was swinging the old denim bag that she always carried.

"Sure did," she said patting the bag. "It's in here."

Jenny suddenly remembered that she needed a spool of thread from the fabric shop. "Cybele, I must stop in this store."

"OK." Cybele said. "I'll go sit in the car."

On the way home, Jenny asked, "What color is your dress?"

Cybele replied, "Blue of course. That's my favorite color."

"Aren't you goin' to show it to me?"

"I'd rather not. Wait until Sunday and you'll see it on me."

Sunday morning dawned bright and sunny. Jed got up earlier on Sunday than any day of the week. He, Ike, Sam and Junie had to work as fast as they could in order to milk the cows and do the other morning chores. Jed rushed in at 9:15 to shower and shave. He and Jenny arrived at church just as the bell in the steeple was giving forth its last ring.

Assembly for Sunday School was beginning as Jenny looked for Thomas and Cybele. She saw them and motioned for Jed to follow her. They slipped into their seats and Milton Eubanks the superintendent announced the first song.

After Sunday School the congregation settled down for the 11:00 preaching service.

Jenny sat by Cybele. "You look lovely in your new dress and white sandals. I like your hair pulled back and tied with that blue scarf."

Jed sat on the platform with Thomas. After the singing of several favorite hymns, the opening prayer and announcements, Jed introduced Thomas as their new pastor.

Thomas stepped confidently behind the podium. "My wife and I are very happy that the Lord has led us to this place. We are very comfortable in our new home. We look forward to getting to know each of you personally."

"My sermon today is going to be my testimony. I think it will acquaint you with me and explain what I believe and why I believe it. Turn in your Bibles to Hebrews 13: 5 and 6. 'Let your conversation be without covetousness: and be content with such things as ye have: for he hath said, I will never leave thee, nor forsake thee. So that we may boldly say, "The Lord is my helper, and I will not fear what man shall do unto me." I like to think of these verses as being my verses. They sum up what the Lord has taught me after many frustrating years of unhappiness, loneliness and the very depth of hell." He took a deep breath, cleared his throat and continued.

"I was born in Chicago. My father did not survive the depression. He owned a small restaurant, one that was chosen by a gang of criminals as a hang out. According to my mother, he tried to resist, but times were hard and he finally gave in to them. When the police moved in on the gang, they shot it out and my father was killed by a policeman's bullet. This happened about a month before I was born. When I was about a year old, my mother married again. Without a doubt, she married the meanest man in the world. From the time I could remember I was beaten, kicked, cursed, shut in a room without food for days at a time. He was just as mean to my mother as he was to me. When I was seven years old, he came in one night drunk as usual. He began to beat on me and I guess my mother had all she could take. She grabbed a butcher knife and stabbed him in the back. I shall never forget how his blood spurted out from the wound." Thomas stopped for a second and wiped his head with his handkerchief. The congregation was very quiet.

He cleared his throat and continued to speak. "My mother was charged with manslaughter. She was sentenced to life in prison. She was there only a short time before she took pneumonia and died. I was sent to live with an aunt and uncle in a small town in Ohio. I stayed with them until I was a teenager. It was in their home that I was first exposed to any sort of religious belief. However, when I say religion, I mean just that. It was a home and church that was strict in the sense that it was run by a set of rules. But there was no love of Jesus Christ mentioned in either place. In fact it was not founded on Jesus, but was based on fear of God. A fear that one would never measure up to God's standards. I was constantly reminded that because of the sins of my parents, I would probably never be one of God's family. So, one day I pretended to go to school, but instead I went to the freight yard and when no one was looking, I slipped into a boxcar on a train headed west. I had my lunch money which was $.25 and $2.00 in pennies that I had saved by returning soda pop bottles I had found. I only had one pair of shoes and they were on my feet. I had hidden my other pair of blue jeans and shirt inside my worn corduroy jacket. I had a snap shot of my mother and father that my aunt and uncle did not know I had kept. I was thirteen years old and ready to make my own way in the world."

Before continuing, Thomas took a drink of water from the glass on the podium. "The next time the train stopped, a big Black fellow slipped into the same boxcar I was in. I was hiding back in the darkest corner in some hay, but he saw me anyway. After the train was rolling again, he came over and looked down at me and I thought my time had come! He reached down and pulled me up and held me out at arms length and began to laugh. He said in a booming voice, 'You ain't nothin' but a little boy. What you doin' actin' like a hobo?' I told him I was thirteen and old enough to leave home. He gently put me down. He sat down and shared his food with me. We talked and I told him all about my life. He shook his head and said, 'Boy, you need somebody and you need em' bad to look after you.' I told him, I didn't need anybody. And he said that we all need somebody. He said there was somebody who cared for me. I told him I didn't believe it. He went on to tell me that God loved me and cared what happened to me. He sang songs to me about Jesus. What he had to say didn't make much impression on me then. But his words have come back again and again since then."

"I arrived in Los Angeles after many days of freight train hopping. I spent a lot of nights with rough neck hobos. The Black man was my constant companion and no one dared harm me. He left me just after we arrived. He had left home because he was tired of the responsibility of a large family and he was not about to tie himself up with a thirteen year old kid. Of course it wasn't long until I was caught stealing food. I became a ward of the court. They notified my uncle in Ohio and he told them I was beyond help and they could do with me as they wished. I was placed in foster home after foster home. I ran away from most. Then God in His infinite mercy looked down on me and sent me to a man that was to become my 'Spiritual Father'. He was Jerry Hill, a young minister that ran a home for boys like myself. He never pressured me to become a Christian. But I saw in his life what I would like my life to be. He sent me to school. I remember how happy he was when I received my high school diploma. The Korean War was raging at that time and I was drafted into the Army. It wasn't long before I was sent to Korea. There I met a lovely young South Korean girl. She was Christian and worked in a mission hospital. We were married by an American missionary. My! How we had great plans. After the war I'd get out of the Army and I'd come and work at the mission."

Thomas swallowed hard, as if the memory were almost too much for him. "But God's ways are not our ways. He is sovereign and things we want often are not what we should have." He paused, drew a long breath and continued. "I was sent to the front lines. In the horror of the war, I was kept alive by the memory of the few months of the greatest happiness I had ever known. I knew if I died, I'd go to heaven, but Oh! how I wanted to live. I was wounded in the leg and sent to an Army hospital about fifty miles from the mission. I sent word for my wife to come to visit me. One day I was told I had a visitor. It was the missionary that had married us. I asked him where was my wife? He told me that a communist had slipped into the mission compound and had thrown a bomb into a section of the hospital and a fire had broken out. My wife was injured by the blast, but managed to rescue three children from the flames. She had lost so much blood, she died within the hour. I really thought my world had crumbled. Not only had I lost her, but our unborn child." Thomas sighed and sucked in his breath as if recalling the experience was almost too much for him.

The audience sat hushed. Some shook their heads in sympathy.

He began again. "How I wished to die. I begged God to let me die. Everyone I had ever loved had died, why couldn't I? But you know, that is one prayer that the Lord did not answer. I left the hospital in Korea and returned to the States. I was bitter and completely without hope of ever being happy again. I was released from the Army. I had no desire to go to school or even to work. Physically I was fine, but mentally I was tortured. I drank, I bummed around with the wrong crowd. I stopped attending church. I was a complete wreck. For some strange reason, I know now it was the hand of the Lord, I decided to go see the man I had lived with during high school. He had written to me all the time I was in the Army. When I arrived, he told me he had been praying for me that day. I found myself pouring out my heart to him—telling him of my doubts that God loved me, even the doubt that there really was a God."

He said, "Tommy, have you ever read the book of Job?"

My reply was no, sir.

"It's time you did, and I'm sure you'll see yourself."

"I spent the remainder of the day in his home, reading and pondering and finally was able to pray. I asked the Lord to forgive me for my doubts and for my sins. To make of me a new person and to show me the plan he had for my life."

"Jerry Hill asked me to stay there with him to help out the younger boys. He counseled me daily, prayed with me and taught me from the Bible. It wasn't long until the Lord showed me that I should go to college under the G. I. Bill. I was a day student at a local college and made my home with Jerry and the boys. The Lord opened doors for me, leading me to the right people and the right influences. After about two years of general college, I went to the same Bible school from which Jerry had graduated. When I finished Bible school I began to work with young people."

"I would go out to the beach and walk up and down in my bathing suit and talk with young people and you'd be surprised at how often I found boys and girls that had run away from home just as I did. I would tell them that God loved them. That God had a plan for their lives. Many times I was jeered at, had rocks and beer cans thrown at me. Sometimes I'd have to run for my life. But in the once in a while times when one of them would listen and ask questions and come to know Christ in a real way, the bad times were worth it. In the late 60's when the drug culture, the hippie movement, the flower children and such like came into focus, the Lord began to lead me into a really useful ministry. With the aid of Jerry, we set up a small center for young people in need. We not only fed them spiritual food, but we helped them find jobs, medical aid or got them into drug or alcohol rehabilitation centers. Recall the Scripture—Matthew 25:40, 'Inasmuch as ye have done it unto one of the least of these my brethren, ye have done it unto me.' We had that on a big plaque over the door to our old converted Army barracks."

"For the last year or so, I had been exercised of the Lord to get into a more settled way of life. I was beginning to feel that young people were noticing how bald I had become and perhaps were saying, what does a fellow his age know about the problems of today's youth."

"In all these years I had never married again. About eight months ago, the Lord sent a lovely ray of sunshine into my life. I was walking along the beach one evening about sunset. I heard a guitar and a soft voice singing.

For a second I thought it was an angel. It had a heavenly sound. And then I saw her. Sitting on a rock with the surf swirling gently around her feet. Her long hair was blowing in the breeze. The evening sun reflected in the water and cast shadows making a yellow glow around her head. She continued to play and sing as I stood transfixed in her presence. When she realized she had an audience, she stopped and smiled at me and my heart melted. Since the death of my wife twenty years ago, I had never had any romantic thoughts of any woman. I had truly devoted my life to the Lord. I complimented her on her music and introduced myself. She told me her name—Cybele Bromley. We walked along the beach until it was dark. When I dropped her at the camp where she was staying I knew she was going to be my wife. It took some convincing, as you see I'm no prize." He laughed before continuing.

"Cybele and I were married about six months ago. I truly feel it was the Lord's will that I sent an application to you and was called as your pastor. My goal is to serve you as the Lord leads. I am open to suggestions and criticism. There is a difference you know."

"I am experienced in pastoral counseling and my door is open to you any hour of the day or night."

After a brief pause he said, "Let us pray. My Lord and my God, my wife and I are here to serve you among these dear people. We ask for your guidance, we plead for your will to be done. We give you thanks and praise, in the name of Jesus, Amen."

He stepped from the pulpit, took Cybele by the hand and walked down the aisle to the vestibule. They stood there until the last person had filed by and shook their hands.

Thomas squeezed Cybele's hand and asked, "Well, what do you think? Do they like us?"

"Of course, but did you have to tell all that stuff about how we met?"

"You're just shy, Cybele. Have I told you today how beautiful you look in that blue dress. Sure was nice of Jenny to buy it for you."

"Shhhh-" Cybele cautioned—"Remember you're not to mention it to her or Jed."

As Jenny and Jed drove home, they were very quiet.

Jenny broke the silence. "Quite a testimony that preacher has. I'm so glad that he has Cybele, especially since he lost his first wife. Didn't she look pretty in that new blue polyester dress?"

"That the one you helped her pick out when you all went shoppin' on Friday? It's a big improvement over those old blue jeans she's been wearin'," Jed replied.

"Funny thing, Jed, when we were shoppin' we saw Vera Gray and while we were catchin' up on all that had been goin' on while she was in Europe, Cybele slipped away and got that dress all by herself. Wouldn't even show it to me. Had it crammed down in that old bag she carries. She's a little different from what I'm used to, but she is a sweet little thing."

CHAPTER 6

THE SETH THOMAS clock on the mantle in the den struck three loud gongs as the front door opened and a cheerie voice called -"Mom, Dad, I'm home."

Jenny jumped up from the couch where she had been taking a nap. "JoAnna, hello, we're in here."

JoAnna with her long red hair pulled back in a pony tail glided into the room. Her skin had turned a lovely shade of brown from being in the sunshine and fresh air at the camp. Brown eyes sparkled as she placed a kiss on the forehead of her father.

"How's my baby girl," Jed asked affectionately.

I'm feelin' great! I had a good time, but I'm glad to be home," she said as she squeezed her mother around the waist. "How's Duke? Has he missed me?"

"Junie took such good care of him, he hasn't had time to miss you," Jed teased.

"I know he needs riding. Let me run upstairs with this stuff and change my clothes and take a quick ride."

"Be careful with him, JoAnna. It's awfully hot today," Jed warned.

"I'll fix you a cold glass of lemonade while you change," Jenny said.

"Hum, that sounds good to me, too," Jed said, patting Jenny lovingly on the arm as she walked past him. His long heavy body was stretched the full length of his Lazy-Boy reclining chair.

JoAnna came bouncing down the stairs, "Mother, has someone slept in my room while I've been gone?"

"Oh, I forgot to tell you," Jenny replied. "Our new pastor and his wife arrived this week and they spent the night with us, but they slept in the guest room."

"Well, someone has been in my room. I can tell."

"Probably that dog of theirs," Jenny sighed.

"They have a dog?"

"A monster is a better description," Jenny said.

"Now Jen," Jed said, "Remember, Czar is a young dog and not settled like our Lady."

"What kind?" JoAnna asked.

"Doberman, solid black. Really a beautiful animal," Jed replied.

JoAnna went out to the barn that had been built especially for her horse. She climbed on the gate to the fence beside the barn and whistled. She heard a soft whinny and the thump of hooves even before the beautiful chestnut brown horse appeared.

"Oh! Duke, how I missed you!" JoAnna said as she stroked his soft coat. "Did you miss me? Looks like Junie has taken good care of you. Ready for a ride?"

She went inside the barn and brought out the bridle and saddle. Duke stood quietly as his mistress bridled and saddled him. She swung into the saddle with ease and Duke started off in a slow trot.

She rode down the lane between the green pastures. She saw the cows near the stream trying to keep cool and away from the flies.

"Duke, this is where I really belong. Out here in the open air riding you. You know, I really dread going away to college this Fall." She breathed deeply. "If time could stand still, I'd have right now to be forever. Just you and me riding along in green fields and never coming to an end."

She turned the horse around and said to him, "Let's have a little work-out. I know it's hot, but you won't mind." She dug her heels into his sides. He got the message and began to run back toward the barnyard. She pulled him to a slower pace as they came near the barn. She turned him to the right and trotted down the road to Ike Wade's house.

Junie Wade was sitting on the porch reading an animal medical book. He jumped quickly to his feet as he saw JoAnna approach.

"So you got back from camp and -takin' ol' Duke for a little ride," Junie said. His face lit up as his wide mouth smiled, revealing even white teeth.

"Wanted to thank you for taking such good care of him" JoAnna said. "Did you ride him any?"

"Oh! Yes, mam. He certainly is one fine ridin' horse," Junie replied.

"When I go away to college this Fall, you'll have to ride him every day."

"Yes, mam, that will be my pleasure."

"Better go now. See you later, Junie. Thanks again for taking care of Duke."

"See you, mam."

As she rode away, Sam Wade came out the door. He was dressed in light green slacks and bright printed long sleeved knit shirt. His high heeled green and brown shoes made him even taller. He towered over his younger brother, mocking him in a drawl, "Yes, mam, no mam. When you gonna come off that stuff little brother? Don't you know that Black dudes like us no longer have to bow and scrape to white women?

All that old mam this and mam that is out and out to stay, man. What I'd like to do to that horse lover, JoAnna Bentley wouldn't be nice to say in front of kids like you."

Junie never replied. He picked up his book and continued to read.

JoAnna carefully put Duke back in the pasture and returned to the house.

The afternoon passed quickly and it was time for church.

Jenny proudly introduced JoAnna to Cybele and Thomas.

"Mother told me about you. Also that you have a dog," JoAnna said to Cybele.

"Yes, a very lovely Doberman," Cybele replied. "And you have a horse."

"That's right. Duke is really a great horse. I've had him about two years. He's won several blue ribbons for me."

"Horse shows, sounds like fun," Cybele replied. "I've never been to one."

"Then I'll have to take you real soon. There will be a big one in Langdon on the 4th of July," JoAnna said.

"It's a date," Cybele smiled.

On the way home from church, Jenny said, "JoAnna, you must be good for Cybele. Her whole personality seemed to change when she was talkin' to you. I guess she would naturally communicate better with younger folks than with me."

"Now Mom, you're not that old!" JoAnna said teasingly. "I would like to get to know her better."

JoAnna looked around the room that had been hers since she was three. The decorations had been changed many times to suit the age of the little girl, now grown up. To the people around her, JoAnna appeared to be a tomboy. But her bedroom reflected a young lady, that despite her love of horses, was very feminine. The four poster white wooden bed held up a light green gingham canopy. It matched the bouffant bedspread and priscilla curtains. The wallpaper was tiny rose buds and the carpet a white shag. JoAnna sat down in the antique rocker in which her grandmother Bentley had rocked her children and she and Jason had been rocked. She opened her Bible and turned to the book of Psalms. She read a while and sat quietly for a few minutes meditating. She closed her eyes and prayed silently. Upon opening her eyes, she noticed something sticking out from under the green gingham pillow sham on the bed. Reaching over, JoAnna pulled out a card with a strange picture on it. "Wonder where this came from," she said out loud. She turned the worn card over and over in her hands.

"Looks sort of like an ordinary playing card. Certainly is old and worn out. Still can't figure out where it came from." She put it in a drawer beside the bed and walked over to the window.

"It's such a beautiful night. The sky is full of stars and the moon is so bright. Almost wish I could go for a ride on Duke in the moonlight." She looked toward the tenant house. She strained her eyes—"Do I see Aunt Temple in the yard with someone? I believe it is. I can't tell who is with her, looks like a woman and a dog. Hum -They are going toward the woods at the back of the house. That's strange—what is Aunt Tempie doing out at night? I'll have to tell Junie about this."

She got into bed. "It is good to be home and in my own bed again. I guess I'm not really the camping type after all."

CHAPTER 7

JULY 4TH WAS an exciting day for the town of Langdon. The mayor and aldermen had gone all out to put on an old fashioned celebration. Nearly everyone in the county was in town to take part. There was a variety of contests. One was to see who could catch the greased pig. Another was to determine who could eat the most watermelon. There was a parade with floats, decorated bicycles, prancing horses, the high school band with its pretty baton twirlers and the county officials riding in a black convertible. The highlight of the day was the horse show.

Jed, Ike and the boys finished milking the cows early. Jed gave them the day off, reminding them that evening milking would begin at 5:00.

JoAnna backed the pickup truck up to the horse trailer. Jed fastened the hook. Junie brought Duke out of the barn. He had helped JoAnna curry the coat of the beautiful animal. The saddle and bridle were cleaned and the polished brass gleamed in the sunlight.

JoAnna was dressed in light green jeans with figured matching blouse. Her red hair fell from beneath a beige western hat. Her boots were spit-polished.

JoAnna drove the pickup. Junie rode with her. Jed and Jenny went in the VW bus and picked Cybele and Thomas up on their way to Langdon.

Thomas had gone the day before to the fair grounds where the 4th of July festivities were being held. He had set up a booth and put up a sign that read "Love-In." Inside he had put up large pictures of beautiful scenery that had Scripture verses on them. Also pictures of happy faces of children and adults. For everyone stopping by to see what was meant by "Love-In", he had a tract for them that said, "Smile, God Loves You." Inside the tract was a Gospel message telling the reader how he could know of God's Love. He had Christian pamphlets, books, and Bible correspondence courses to offer to anyone interested.

It was a beautiful day. There had been a shower the night before leaving everything fresh and green. The 4th of July celebration was almost as important to the folks of Langdon as the county fair. It was a time to visit with friends and to renew acquaintances of the past. The young folks participated in the contests while the older folks reminisced of days gone by.

Cybele had brought along her battered guitar. She sat on a stool inside the booth and strummed a tune. In a sweet soft voice, she sang about God's love, about His love for mankind in sending His only Son in the person of Jesus Christ to redeem fallen man.

Several people stopped by the "Love-In" booth. Sam Wade and his friends Jock and Zelda stopped by.

"Hello, Mrs. Wilson," Sam drawled. "Remember me?"

Cybele looked up from her guitar. "Sure, I remember you. You and your brother brought my dog home when he ran away." She stepped outside the booth.

"I'm Sam. Sam Wade. These are my friends Zelda and Jock." "Nice to meet you," Cybele said, extending her hand to each of them.

"We brought Aunt Tempie with us today," Sam said. "Have you seen her around?"

"What? Who is Aunt Temple?" Cybele asked.

Jock and Zelda began talking to Thomas about some of the pamphlets he was offering.

"Come on now, Mrs. Wilson, you know my Aunt Tempie. You spend enough time with her and all her old herb medicines. What have you two been conjurin' up by the light of the moon?" Sam smiled a broad smile showing even white teeth.

"I don't know what you are talking about Mr. Wade." Cybele replied. She looked deep into his dark eyes.

Sam suddenly felt an icy chill run over his body. Realizing he had struck on something that Cybele did not want to discuss, he excused himself, forgetting about Jock and Zelda.

Cybele decided to go for a walk. She walked by all the booths. She bought a candy apple and sunk her teeth into the sweet sticky coating. She walked out behind the booths and flung herself onto the soft green grass. The grass felt cool and refreshing. She munched the apple.

"Miz Cybele, how are you today?"

Cybele looked up. Peering down at her from beneath a faded straw hat was a wrinkled black face. A pair of oval shaped wire rimmed glasses were perched on the flat nose. Signs of snuff oozed from the corners of the wrinkled thick lips.

"Hi!" Cybele replied, looking around to see if anyone was in sight.

"What yo doin' way out here by yoself?" Aunt Tempie asked.

"Just wanted to be by myself for a minute," Cybele replied.

"I knows what yo mean, chil'. Us folks that has er—special powers, we'se jest gotta go git to ourselves sometimes." She rolled her black eyes. "I knows yo has the power. I can feel it in my bones when I'm near you. I knowed it the fust time I ever laid these ol' eyes on yo. I'd been wonderin' what was goin' ter happen when I dies, and her' you come along to take my place."

Cybele got up. "Aunt Tempie, I don't think it's a good idea if we're seen together. Sam is already suspicious. I wouldn't want my husband to find out. He wouldn't understand."

"Chil', when is yo ever gonna tell him. Hit's no shame to have special powers, if'n yo use 'em right. Of course, folks always think you're crazy, but that's because most of 'em is jealous. They all wish they could see into the future or heal folks of ailments or cause certain things to happen by and by. You jist stick with ol' Aunt Tempie and you'll be some gran folks some day."

Cybele ran toward the area where the horses were. She didn't look back.

"Cybele", JoAnna called. "Come over and wish Duke and me, good luck."

"Oh! You'll win without my wishes. But good luck anyway." Cybele patted Duke on the nose.

Duke let out a long whinny and reared up on his hind legs pawing the air with his fore feet.

JoAnna and Cybele jumped back and away from the flying hooves.

"Duke, what's wrong?" JoAnna shouted.

"He must not like me!" Cybele exclaimed. She moved away.

Junie grabbed the reins and in a calm gentle voice talked soothing words to the trembling animal.

"Junie, why do you suppose Duke did such a thing?" JoAnna asked.

"Only time I ever saw Duke act like that was one time while you was gone to camp. I rode him over to our house and Aunt Tempie was sittin' on the front porch. I rode him right up to the end of the porch so she could pat him. When she touched him, he reared up and almost threw me off and he took off in a run and it was hard for me to control him."

"Does your Aunt Tempie know Cybele?" JoAnna asked.

"I don't think so,' Junie replied. "Why do you ask?"

"I just wondered," JoAnna said ponderingly.

A voice came over the loud speaker—"It is now time for the horse show. All entries line up at the North gate."

"That's us Duke," JoAnna said as she swung into the saddle.

"I'll be rootin' for you," Junie said with a big smile.

The day ended with a blue ribbon for Duke and JoAnna. Thomas went home with empty boxes and many names and addresses of people interested in finding out more about the love of Jesus Christ. Jenny had heard all about what kind of clothes would be fashionable for Fall from Vera Gray. And who might be Vera's next romance. Jed had talked crops and cows and the latest in farm equipment with nearly every man in the county.

Cybele was very quiet all the way home. She said she had a headache and was very tired and wouldn't be going back at 9:00 for the fireworks. Jenny and Jed agreed with her that the day had been long enough for them.

"Well, you can all stay home, but I'm going to see the fireworks," Thomas said as he got out of Jed's VW. "I've always enjoyed fireworks.

Guess it's a hang over from my childhood." Thomas left home at 8:30. Cybele and Czar went into the kitchen. Cybele got out her ouija board.

"I haven't had time to consult you recently," she said out loud. "Thomas told me to throw you away. But I can't." She patted the board lovingly. "When I touch you I feel so close to my Aunt Phoebe. I can still hear her voice saying, 'Honey, I give you my treasures because you're the one that can carry on. You have powers you've never even discovered.' And now today, to have Aunt Tempie tell me the same thing. Oh! Aunt Phoebe what does it all mean?"

"I know, I'll ask the Ouija board."

She placed her finger tips on the pointer and closed her eyes. In a soft voice she asked, "Ouija, tell me what powers I have."

The pointer began to move. Cybele opened her eyes. The round hole in the middle of the pointer began to stop over certain letters. Cybele spelled them out loud"-PSYCHIC—Psychic, Psychic powers! Now that's too much! Tell me more, Ouija." She pressed her finger tips hard on the pointer. It moved about the board. Cybele spelled out loud—"BEWARE OF JOANNA—Beware of JoAnna' Why should I? She's my friend. In fact she's about the only one in Langdon that I feel close to."

While Cybele sat pondering what this could mean, Czar got up from under the table and began walking back and forth in front of the back door. He stopped and looked at Cybele and let out a loud howl. It was such a weird sharp sound, it made goose pimples break out on Cybele's arms. She opened the screen door. He bounded out. He ran toward the church. By the light of the full moon she saw him run into the graveyard.

Suddenly, Cybele saw the car lights turning into the driveway.

"Better not let Thomas see you," She grabbed the ouija board and quickly shoved it into the linen closet in the hall. There it lay, safe, underneath a pair of new sheets that Vera Gray had given her.

CHAPTER 8

JULY WAS VERY hot. The thermometer hovered around 95 degrees in the day time and in the high 80's during the night. The humidity was 100%. Thunder storms, especially at night were prevalent.

One hot humid evening Jenny, JoAnna and Vera Gray were invited to Cybele's house. The four were knitting baby sweaters for missionaries. Jed had gone with Thomas to visit some of the people that had been reached through the July 4th "Love-In" booth.

Jenny chattered away about how many packages of vegetables she had put in her freezer, how many pickles she had made and how much jelly was stashed away in the pantry for winter.

Vera told Jenny that she worked too hard and she should take vacation and go with her on a shopping spree to Atlanta.

Cybele served then lemonade and granola cookies.

"Why Cybele these cookies are delicious." Jenny drawled.

"I'm getting to be quite a cook, thanks to you," Cybele replied. "I'm a real health food nut. I found a little health food store over in Rockvale that has all sorts of organic grown foods, several different kinds of flour and every spice and herb you ever heard of. Do either of you ever shop there?"

"Never been there," Vera answered. "Matter of fact, I don't do much cooking. Since my husband died, I do a lot of eating out."

"I know you miss him," Jenny said sympathetically. "He was such a fine person."

"I do indeed," Vera sighed. "When my first husband died, I thought life was over for me, and then to lose my second husband was almost too much for me." She stopped knitting and closed her eyes as if she were fighting back tears. "Sometimes I feel like he really isn't gone. You know he always claimed to have E.S.P.—and sometimes, especially at night I almost feel his presence. I catch myself calling his name."

Suddenly, a streak of bright lightning flashed, lighting the sky like thousands of flashing neon lights. The thunder loudly rumbled. It began to rain hard. The wind blew the curtains in Cybele's living room. She dropped her knitting and ran to close the windows on the Southeast side of the house.

Another streak of lightning split the sky. As the thunder boomed out like heavy kettle drums, every light in the house went out.

"My, my," Jenny shrieked. "Must have struck a power line nearby."

"I'll bring some candles," Cybele called from the hall. She scratched around in the linen closet. "Wow, it's dark in here. Where will I ever find a match?"

"I have some in my purse," Vera replied, feeling around on the couch until she found it. She struck one as Cybele handed her a candle.

"Now where did I put those candle holders?" Cybele said. She opened a drawer in one of the end tables and brought out a wrought iron candle holder. She placed the candle in the holder and set it on the coffee table.

"What a quaint candle holder!" Vera exclaimed. Wherever did you get it? It's shaped like some sort of monster with the candle sticking in its mouth."

"Oh! My Aunt Phoebe gave it to me many years ago," she answered quickly.

"It's so unusual, I'd display it all the time if I were you," Vera said.

"I can't, Thomas doesn't like it. Looks like the storm is subsiding a little. Wonder how long the power will be off?"

JoAnna mused out loud, "A black candle, that's what witches burn."

Jenny laughed. "Vera, remember those candles you brought me from Williamsburg. They were black. JoAnna never would let me burn them. She read someplace where witch and devil worshipers use them."

"Mother, where are those candles?" JoAnna asked. "I was looking in the box they came in the other day and they were gone."

"I haven't any idea," Jenny replied. "They were there the last time I looked in the upstairs hall closet."

"Mother, you and I really should go on home. I need to check on Duke. Sometimes he gets sort of nervous during a storm." JoAnna said.

"Yes, we'd better do that. Seems like it isn't rainin' quite so hard now. Vera, will you stay here with Cybele until Thomas and Jed get back?"

"Sure, I just had my hair done today and I'm not about to get it wet," Vera replied, patting her blond curls.

The women exchanged good-byes and Jenny and JoAnna ran to their car between flashes of lightning.

"Vera," Cybele spoke. "Did your late husband really have E.S.P.?"

"I don't know for sure," Vera answered thoughtfully. "He used to say things, like if the phone rang, he'd say that will be so and so. And sure enough it was always whoever he named. I'd tease him about it. He would laugh and say that it was E.S.P. The day he died, he said I'll be gone at 6:00 p. m. And he died at 5 minutes 'til 6." She took a lace trimmed handkerchief from her purse and daintily blew her nose.

"Vera," Cybele said in a soft voice, "Have you ever had the desire to communicate with your husband?"

"Cybele, you don't mean talk to someone who is dead?"

"Yes, that's just what I mean. You know it's possible."

"Oh! You're puttin' me on," Vera drawled.

"No, I'm not. It is possible to talk to our departed loved ones. I've spoken to my Aunt Phoebe and to my grandmother many times."

"You have? But how is that possible?" Vera asked, leaning forward to catch her every word.

"You have to believe," Cybele whispered.

"Believe what?" Vera asked.

"Believe that it's possible to talk to the dead."

"When could we try it?" Vera asked eagerly.

"When would you like?" Cybele replied.

"Soon as possible," Vera retorted.

"I'll have to do same planning and consulting," Cybele said thoughtfully. "I'll need something that belonged to Mr. Gray."

"We could do it at our house. His library is full of everything that belonged to him. Books, papers, even his pipe is where he left it. Oh! this is so excitin'! Could we have anyone else present? How about Jenny?"

"I don't think so," Cybele replied. "We'd just better let this be our little party. And please don't say anything to Thomas."

"Cybele," Vera said. "You've never told me very much about yourself. Where are you from originally and I believe Thomas said he met you in California. What were you doing there?"

"I'm from New Orleans. I went to California to study art. I liked it there so well, made so many friends, I stayed until I was married. Never have been back to Louisiana." With her eyes closed she leaned her head back against the chair.

The black candle flickered, casting weird shadows on the wall.

Vera shivered. "I believe this rain is coolin' things off. I'll be glad when the power comes back on."

Headlights of an approaching automobile cast light through the window.

"Must be Thomas and Jed," Vera said.

The door opened and as the two men strode into the room, the electricity came on.

Cybele quickly blew out the candle and set it and the holder behind her chair.

"Bad electrical storm," Jed said.

"Jenny and JoAnna went on home to check on Duke. I'll drive you home, Jed," Vera said. "It's been a delightful evening, Cybele."

"Yes, it has been for me too," Cybele replied. "See you soon."

Vera and Jed got into her light blue Cadillac.

"This is some automobile, Vera," Jed said.

"Mr. Gray always wanted me to have the very best of everything."

"He sure did. He really was a fine gentleman with a good head for business," Jed replied.

"Yes, a fine man," Vera said thoughtfully as she steered the car through the rain. The lightening flickered like the blink of an eye. "Wonder how life would have been for me had I not gone away to Sullins College. Remember, I left for school the same week you went into the army^"

"I remember," Jed said, looking toward Vera. "It's been over 25 years, but seems only yesterday."

"I wonder, if Jenny hadn't been the girl in your life in high school, if I'd had a chance."

Jed laughed, "I remember how all those fellows always hung around you. You never had any time for a country boy like me."

"Jed, is that what you really thought? And all this time I've never really forgiven Jenny for capturing the handsomest fellow in the county."

"Well, it's time you forgave her. Besides, if you'd married a poor dairy farmer like me you'd never have been drivin' a car like this."

They arrived in front of the big white frame house.

"Thanks for the lift," Jed called as he got out of the car.

"Good night, Jed," Vera said. "Remember, there will always be a special place in my heart for you. And for Jenny too," she added.

CHAPTER 9

AUGUST 1ST WAS an exciting day in the Bentley household. Jenny, Jed and JoAnna left at 10:00 to drive the thirty miles to the airport.

The whisper jet glided to a halt, the steps were lowered and the second person down was a tall red-headed young man. His face and arms were tan. He blinked in the bright sunlight and then he saw the three people waiting for him.

JoAnna reached him first and threw her arms around him.

Jenny grabbed him next. Her eyes filled with tears of happiness.

Jed shook hands and lovingly slapped him on the back. "Welcome home, son."

It's good to be home," Jason replied.

After picking up Jason's luggage, they made their way to the parking lot.

"Dad, I'll drive," Jason said. "It will be so good to drive on a wide straight paved road. Where I've been the trails are only wide enough for a two wheeled cart drawn by a donkey. Mom, I hope you've cooked some good food. I've eaten so many sweet potatoes, I hope I never see another one."

"Jason, I believe you've lost weight. But I'll see to it that you have plenty to eat," Jenny said.

"Tell us more about your experiences," JoAnna urged.

"I can say one thing," Jason began, "I'm glad the Good Lord allowed me to be born in the United States. Of course there are big modern cities, but where we were working was the rural areas. Dad, you wouldn't believe how primitive they farm."

"I've seen enough pictures in magazines to be glad that I live here," Jed answered.

"Mom, I'm sorry, I never had time to write many letters while I was gone. I really appreciated hearing all the news from you. The new preacher and his wife and their dog sound interesting."

"They are very interesting," JoAnna said emphatically nodding her head and making a face.

"And what does that mean, JoAnna?" Jason asked.

"I'll leave that for you to decide for yourself," JoAnna answered. "But I have my suspicions about anyone that burns black candles."

"Black candles?" Jason said. "JoAnna, you've been reading too many books about vampires again. Remember when we were kids, you used to read about witches, and monsters after you went to bed at night and you'd get so scared you'd have to come get in bed with me."

"I remember, I guess I've always feared the occult. Now that I'm a Christian, I know that I'm not to have anything to do with the powers of darkness. Satan is the ruler of that world and I serve the Lord, not Satan," JoAnna answered thoughtfully.

"In the village where I've been living, there was a great deal of demon worship. The other fellows on the agricultural team and I attended Sunday services at a mission station run by a couple from Florida. They have run into a lot of resistance to the Gospel by these people whose culture is wrapped up in idol worship. JoAnna, I saw same real live witch doctors."

JoAnna shuddered. "Poor lost souls. They don't know that Christ died for their sins."

The trip home was very pleasant. Each member of the Bentley family sharing in the conversation and laughter. Times like these, when the family was all together, were very precious to Jenny.

Jason began working with his father on the dairy farm. The men were grateful for his help. Sam Wade was especially glad for his assistance as he was preparing to enter the University. Football practice was beginning the following week. Sam was very happy these days with the prospects of college and a new girl friend. He liked to tease Jason.

"Say Jason, what did the chicks look like in that wild country you spent the summer in?"

Jason answered without smiling. "Sorry, Sam, but I didn't have any time for chick gazing while I was gone."

"Jason, you wouldn't know a real chick if you saw one. Take that new preacher's wife, bet you'd never guess where I saw her one night last week."

Jason looked up from the barn floor that he was hosing down. "What are you talking about?"

Sam laughed, "You're interested, huh! She is an interesting female. Sort of strange though, strange in the same way my Aunt Tempie is strange."

"Where did you see her?"

"With that old dog of course. She never goes any place without him. Wish she'd leave him at home sometime. Would be easier to get acquainted with her. I'm half scared of that mongrel."

"Are you going to tell me where you saw her or am I going to have to squirt you with this hose?"

"Wouldn't try that old buddy. I saw Mrs. Wilson out in the graveyard next to your church. I had been over to Emma Lou Thompsons. On the way home I ran out of gas and had to walk. I took a short cut through the woods and came out at the edge of the graveyard. The moon was full and I could see real good. It was her all right. She was sitting on a grave stone and sort of singing in a soft voice. She didn't see me. I started to speak to her, but that scene seemed sort of spookie-like to me. So, I just continued on my merry way."

"Wonder what she was doing there?" Jason said thoughtfully.

"Beats me," Sam answered. "She's a weird one. She takes walks at night a lot. I know she sometimes comes to see Aunt Tempie at night. Those two probably conjure up some voodoo together." He laughed loudly.

The next day, Jason had the opportunity to meet the Wilsons. Jenny had them over for dinner.

Cybele was usually very quiet, but on this particular evening she was very talkative. Even Thomas noticed and commented about how outgoing she was becoming.

"Must be the company I'm keeping these days," Cybele laughed. She turned to Jason. "Tell us more about your summer. I've always wanted to go to South America."

"I didn't know that," Thomas said. "Perhaps we should apply for missionary work down there.

Cybele patted Thomas' bald head. There are allot of things about me that you don't know my dear."

The telephone rang. JoAnna answered.

"It's for you, Thomas. It's Mrs. Greene. Her husband just had a severe heart attack. They've taken him to the county hospital and she'd like very much for you to go to the hospital."

"Tell her I'll be right there," Thomas replied.

"I'll go with you Thomas," Jed said. "Henry Greene has been an elder in our church for the last twenty years. Perhaps there is something I can do."

"Jason, will you see that Cybele gets home," Thomas said, "And don't wait up for me, honey."

Jed and Thomas left.

Jenny settled down to mending and watching her favorite TV show.

Jason, JoAnna and Cybele went out to the wide front porch. They sat down and watched the fireflies flitting across the lawn.

"Cybele, did you ever catch lightening bugs and put them in a jar?" Jason asked. "JoAnna and I used to."

"No, I don't think I ever did," she answered. "I lived in the city and there probably weren't enough to go around."

"Cybele, you've never really told us much about your life before you married Thomas." JoAnna said. "Tell us about your childhood."

"Not much to tell," Cybele replied. She got up from the porch swing and went to the steps. Quincy the cat was sprawled on the top step. She reached down to gather him up in her arms. He suddenly raised up on his four legs. His back arched with his tail straight up. He hissed and clawed at Cybele, then suddenly ran away.

"Quincy!" JoAnna exclaimed. "I've never seen you act so rude. He's usually very gentle. Cybele did he scratch you?"

"A little, but its O. K.," she answered. "Guess he doesn't like me any better than he likes Czar. Speaking of Czar, we left him tied in the carport. Guess I'd better go on home and check on him."

"Let me get the car keys," Jason said. "I told Thomas that I'd see that you got home safely."

"Goodnight, Jenny, thanks for a lovely dinner. See you soon JoAnna," Cybele called as she went down the steps.

"You never did tell us much about your childhood," Jason broke the silence as they drove along.

"Let's not talk about me," Cybele replied. "I'd much rather hear about you. What do you plan to do after college?"

"Not quite sure. But after my experience this sunnier, I think I'd like to go into some sort of missionary work. Not only to spread the Gospel, but to teach people how to raise crops properly so they can feed themselves. I saw so much poverty. If I could just teach a few people how to make their farming profitable, then I wouldn't have lived in vain."

"You live in vain? A strong handsome fellow like you hasn't lived in vain." Cybele's voice became high pitched almost as if it were not her voice speaking. "Here we are, home already, please come in. I enjoy talking to you so much."

Jason stopped the car in the driveway and got out.

"So this is your dog?" he asked.

Czar began to jump and strain against the chain that was holding him. He barked a loud throaty bark.

"Is he always this frisky?"

"Not always," Cybele replied.

His friendly bark suddenly turned into a snarling growl. He showed his sharp teeth.

Jason said in a soothing voice, "Now boy, what's all the excitement. Nobody is going to hurt you or your mistress." He started to walk toward the dog. It lunged at him, pulling on the chain.

"Czar, Czar," Cybele scolded. "Behave yourself." The more she said, the more violent the dog's actions became.

Jason retreated to the car. Suddenly the chain snapped. The dog lunged forward running past Cybele and barking loudly. He ran wildly across the church yard and into the graveyard.

Jason stepped from the car. "Wonder what's wrong with him. You don't suppose there has been a prowler about." He looked toward the church.

"It's unusual for Czar to act like that. He's usually so gentle," Cybele declared. She unlocked the front door.

"I'd better come on in with you and have a look around," Jason said.

They went into the dark house. Cybele turned on the light in the living room. "Looks like everything's O. K."

Jason went from room to room peering behind the doors and in closets.

"Guess I'd better go on home," Jason said.

"Please stay," Cybele pleaded. "I have same cold lemonade in the frig."

"O.K. Just for a little while," Jason replied.

Cybele poured two glasses of lemonade.

"Do you have a steady girl friend?" Cybele asked.

"NO, not really," Jason replied. "I've been praying that the Lord would lead me to the right Christian girl."

Cybele gazed thoughtfully at this handsome slender young man sitting across the table from her. He was sitting in the chair where Thomas ordinarily sat. Suddenly she got up and went around the table. She put her hand on Jason's shoulder and leaned forward and kissed him on the forehead.

Jason was embarrassed and stood up. "Why did you do that?" he asked.

"Because you're so special," she replied.

"I'd better go," Jason said.

Cybele sat back down without answering.

Jason slammed the car door and drove away.

Cybele spoke out loud. "Powers of darkness come to me. Make Jason Bentley pay attention to me," In her hands she held a white handkerchief with the letters JB in one corner. She sat quietly fumbling the handkerchief. She was brought back to reality by Czar scratching on the back screen door.

CHAPTER 10

THOMAS WILSON HAD just finished his Sunday morning sermon. After his closing prayer, he walked quickly to the vestibule of the church. He wiped his perspiring bald forehead with his handkerchief. He shook hands with each member as they filed past.

"Good sermon, Pastor," Vera Gray said as she extended him a white gloved hand. "One of these days I'm going to give enough money to this church so it can be air-conditioned."

"Why don't you just do that!" Jenny said, following Vera out into the blazing hot August sun.

"My house is air-conditioned, and why shouldn't I be just as comfortable at church as I am at home?" Vera said. She got into her air conditioned car and drove away.

"She makes me sick," Jenny fumed.

"Who makes you sick?" Jed asked coming up behind her.

"Vera Gray, that's who." Jenny answered.

"Now, now Jenny, after a good sermon like we've just heard you shouldn't get yourself upset," Jed patted her shoulder.

"Vera and her money," Jenny pranced out to the car.

"She's got money all right," Jed said.

They joined JoAnna and Jason in the car.

Jason started the car. As he was backing up, he almost hit a tree.

"Can't you drive, brother?" JoAnna asked sarcastically.

"Better than you," he answered.

"Wasn't that a good sermon?" Jed asked.

"I thought it was lousy," Jason replied. "I thought you said he could preach."

"I thought it was great," JoAnna said.

"I was too hot to really listen," Jenny snorted.

"I suppose you'll want us to spend a bunch of the Lord's money on air-conditioning," Jed answered.

"Vera just told me that one of these days she was going to contribute enough money for it. I'll believe that when I see it. All she thinks about is buying clothes,'" Jenny snorted.

"Maybe you ought to think a little more about clothes," Jed said.

"Jed Bentley, I never knew you noticed," Jenny said angrily.

"I notice more than you think,"

No one else spoke as they drove home.

Lunch was a quiet time. Occasionally JoAnna and Jason bickered.

The telephone rang at 3:00.

"Dad it's for you," JoAnna called.

"Who is disturbing my nap," Jed yawned.

"Hello! Oh! Hello Ike. Is that so," his voice was surlev.

"It's mighty short notice"   "Well, go ahead—we'll make out."

He threw down the phone.

"What was that all about?" Jenny asked.

"It was Ike. He just found out a cousin of his died over in Rockvale and the funeral is at 4:30. That means he won't be here by milkin' time," Jed answered grumpily. "I don't know why he has to go to the funeral."

"Jed, you've always been so understandin'. What's gotten into you?" Jenny asked.

"Gotten into me? There's nothin' wrong with me. It's Ike and you and everybody else." He went out to the front porch, slamming the screen door behind him.

"Well, I never!" Jenny exclaimed. "What is wrong with this family? It must be this humid hot weather."

"I wish I were at the beach," JoAnna said. "I wouldn't mind the heat if I was able to dip in the ocean."

"I wish you were there. Then I wouldn't have to listen to you gripe all the time," Jason said.

"Why, Jason Bentley, I haven't heard you speak to your sister like that in years," his mother scolded.

"I feel like there is something that has a grip on me. Something that makes me say things and do things and even think things that I'd rather not think. I've felt this way ever since I got back from South America."

"Sounds like you need a psychiatrist, big brother," JoAnna chided. "I'm like Mom, I think it's this heat that is getting next to all of us. Soon as we have a break, we'll all see a difference."

"I think there is more to it than the weather," Jason replied. "Better get into my work clothes. It's almost milking time."

"I'll help too," JoAnna said.

Jed, JoAnna and Jason went out to the barn.

"Dad, are you sure it's milking time. There isn't a cow in sight," Jason said.

Jed looked at his watch. "It's 5 o'clock. That's strange. They are usually up here anxious to be milked.

"I'll go down toward the pond and look for them," JoAnna said.

She started down the well-worn path.

Junie came into the barn. "Sorry Mr. Jed, but Pa hasn't come back from the funeral yet. Where's the cows?"

"JoAnna has gone to look for them," Jason replied.

The three men prepared to start the milking.

JoAnna came panting into the barn. "There isn't a cow anywhere around. I've called and called and I haven't even heard one moo! I'm beginning to think they've been rustled."

"Who would rustle milk cows?" Junie asked. "I'll saddle Duke and yo' can ride down to the south pasture and look for 'em."

"This really makes me mad," Jed said angrily. "It's too hot to have to look for cows. I'm tempted to not even look for them. They're the ones who'll suffer."

JoAnna swung into the saddle and rode down the lane. At the heels of the fast pacing horse, ran Lady the collie.

"Lady will find those ornery cows," Junie declared.

Jenny came walking swiftly into the barn calling loudly, "Jed, I just got a telephone call from Bud Smith. He says there are 30 or 40 cows in his corn field and he thought they might be ours. I told him you all were milkin' ours, but I see that you aren't."

"Well, I'll be!" Jed said, stomping his foot. "They must be ours. Our fence must be down on the side of the pasture next to Bud Smith's property. Jason, didn't you and Sam check that fence last week?"

"Yes, sir, we did, and it looked fine to me."

"Well, you must have made a mistake. Come on, it will take all of us to drive them back into the pasture. They've probably ruined Bud's corn by now and eaten so much they'll be sick."

"I'll get the pick up and drive you all over there," Jenny said. "You all will be sick racin' around in this heat."

The men climbed into the back of the truck and Jenny drove them by way of the highway to Bud Smith's farm.

Munching away on the tender ears of corn were all thirty-six of the Bentley herd plus six frisky calves tramping down corn stalks.

JoAnna arrived. "I found the place where the fence is down. Let's try driving them back that way."

Lady was frantically barking and nipping at the heels of the cows. With much shouting and waving of arms the six people including Bud Smith drove the reluctant cows back onto the Bentley property

"This is terrible," Jed said to Bud. "I'm so sorry. I'll be glad to pay for the damage to your corn crop."

"Well, I should think you would, Bentley," he replied in a surly tone as he spat a stream of brown tobacco juice. It landed on an unsuspecting grasshopper that jumped sideways to avoid further damage.

"If'n you'd keep yo' fences repaired, ye old cows wouldn't git out. And that there ol' black dog better quit comin' round here chasin' my chickens."

"What black dog?" Jed asked.

"That ol' black dog that I hear tell belongs to that new preacher that ya'll got at your church. He was out there barkin' at your cows just afore they come bustin' through the fence. I hollered at him and he runned off through the woods."

"Bud you figure up what I owe you and I'll be over tomorrow to pay you," Jed replied as he climbed into the pickup beside Jenny.

"You better tell your preacher what I said 'bout his ol' dog," he shouted and shook his fist in the air.

"I didn't know that Czar was makin' a nuisance of him self in the neighborhood," Jenny declared.

"Sounds like he might be," Jed replied. "I sure don't like the idea of him chasin' our cows. I won't be surprised if that's the reason the cows tore down the fence. I can't believe that the fence was already down. He probably barked and scared them into running against the fence. They must have broken down one of the posts and got right into the corn."

"Ol' Bud sure was mad," Jenny said.

"He's an old grouch anyway," Jed said. "I remember when I was a kid, he was just as mean then as he is now."

"I've always felt sorry for his wife," Jenny said. "She's such a meek little woman. Never gets to go anywhere. Not even to church."

As they drove into the barnyard, Ike came out of the barn.

"Jed, I'm sorry I'm so late. But where are the cows. You ain't finished milkin'?" Ike asked.

"Our cows got out and got in Bud Smith's corn. Junie, Jason and JoAnna are drivin' them up now," Jed replied.

"How was your cousin's funeral?" Jenny asked.

"Sad, sad," Ike replied, shaking his head and rolling his dark eyes. "He was only 50 years old, had a heart attack and died on the way to the hospital. Worst of all, he didn't know the Lord. He had always been a drinkin' man and I reckon it ruined his health. Left a wife and six children. Most of them are about grown. From the looks of some of those boys, they are followin' in their pappy's footsteps."

The sound of voices, the clatter of hooves, the barking of Lady broke the still hot air, as the cows came into the lane outside the barn.

"Time to milk these critters," Jed said. "This has been some Sunday evenin'. Jenny, you and JoAnna better go on to church without us. We'll never make it."

"I'll leave your supper on the table," Jenny said as she started for the house.

Thomas preached for twenty minutes to a small tired looking group. Everyone looked sleepy in the humid atmosphere. He raised his voice and pounded his fist on the podium, realizing his audience was anything but alert.

He spoke on the virtue of true brotherly love. He expounded on Christ's command to "love thy neighbor as thyself." He ended his sermon by asking all to stand and sing "Blest Be the Tie That Binds Our Hearts in Christian Love, the Fellowship of Kindred Minds is like to that Above."

Jenny was the last one out of the church. She had deliberately stayed back so she could have a word with Thomas.

"Where is Cybele tonight?" she asked.

Thomas cleared his throat and his bald head turned a darker crimson than usual. "Cybele, Oh' She has problems, her old life keeps creeping up er—I mean, she decided to stay home. Er—she, I mean we had a little domestic quarrel. Nothing to worry about you know how it is—two people living under the same roof can't always agree on everything."

"You all too?" Jenny said. "This has been one of those days when my whole family has been bickering. We blamed it on the heat, but perhaps that isn't it at all. And to top it off, our cows got out and were in Bud Smith's corn. That's the reason Jed and Jason didn't make it tonight. By the way, Bud Smith said to tell you that your dog has been comin' to his place and chasin' his chickens. He claims he saw Czar chasin' our cows today."

"Hmm," Thomas replied thoughtfully. "I'd better go over and apologize to Mr. Smith. I've been wanting to go to see him and his wife and to be able to witness to them."

"More power to you, preacher. I've never had any luck at that. Bud Smith is a hard nut to crack," Jenny replied.

"I've dealt with hard nuts before," Thomas said. "Thanks for telling me about our dog. I'll see that he is chained when he isn't right with us. Tell Jed that I'm sorry about all his cow problems. Goodnight Jenny, goodnight JoAnna."

CHAPTER 11

JENNY'S PHONE RANG as she was setting the table for lunch.

"Hello, Jenny, this is Vera."

"Hello, Vera," Jenny said coolly.

"Jenny, I just got a call from Cybele and she wants me to come over to her house tonight. She has something special to show me. I was wondering if you'd like to come. I could pick you up around 8 o'clock."

"Oh! I guess so. Jed and Thomas have something planned for tonight. You wasn't at church last night."

"Too hot," Vera replied. "Does seem a bit cooler today."

"I'll see you tonight, thanks for callin'." Jenny returned to her cooking. Jed and Jason came in for lunch.

"Got that fence fixed over by Bud's property," Jed reported as he sat down for lunch. "I wrote him a check for the damage to his corn. Thomas came by as I was leavin'. Ol' Bud was really givin' it to him about his dog chasin' his chickens. Thomas better watch out, Bud Smith is just mean enough to shoot that dog.

"Dad, I've never heard you talk about Mr. Smith that way," Jason said as he buttered three fluffy biscuits.

"Now that you are grown-up, I guess you'll learn for yourself who lives for the devil," Jed replied.

"Yes, I'm learning," Jason said. "I've never talked about this to anyone, but on our college campus last winter there were devil worshipers."

Jenny's mouth flew open. "Jason, you don't mean it!"

"Mom, I'm afraid it's true. I was sitting at a table in the library one day. A fellow across from me was wearing an unusual medallion around his neck. One reason I noticed it was because he kept messing with it and unconsciously hitting it on the book he was reading. The noise sort of irritated me. I guess he sensed I was looking at him. He looked up and our eyes met. I said to him, 'nice medallion you have there.' His eyes seemed to take on a strange glow and he answered, 'ever heard of the Satanic church of America?' I guess I was rather shocked and probably showed it in my face. 'We worship Satan,' he said. 'This medallion is our symbol. Be glad to make an appointment with you to further explain it.'"

"That was the last thing I wanted to hear about, so I replied, 'I've been bought by the blood of Jesus Christ and my faith is in Him, the true and living God.' I reached inside my shirt and pulled out the silver cross that JoAnna gave me last Christmas. That guy took one look at it, slammed his book shut and ran out of the library. I just happened to look down at the book he was reading. It was on witchcraft. Pass the string beans, please."

"Jason," JoAnna spoke thoughtfully, passing the string beans. "Did you ever see that man again?"

"No, I never did," Jason replied between bites of sliced tomatoes. I don't think he was a student."

"Excuse me, please," JoAnna said with excitement in her voice.

"I just remembered something. I've got to run upstairs a minute."

"What was that all about?" Jenny asked as she refilled the iced tea glasses.

JoAnna bounced back into the room. She held a round silver medallion in her hand. "Look Jason, did that medallion look anything like this one?"

Jason took it in his hand and examined it carefully. "I believe it was similar. In fact it looks the same. Where did you get this?"

"Junie gave it to me."

"Where did he get it?"

"He found it near that old log cabin where Aunt Tempie makes her herb medicine. Said he showed it to her and she didn't recall ever seeing it before."

"Wonder who around here has ever had anything to do with the church of Satan," Jed laughed heartily. "I know plenty of folks who are following after the devil, but they don't know anythin' about a church."

"Do these people actually worship Satan in a church service like we worship the Lord in ours?" Jenny asked.

"Mom, I'm sure they do," Jason replied seriously.

"Whatever is this world comin' to," Jenny declared shaking her head.

"What should I do with this thing?" JoAnna asked looking at the medallion. "Now that I know what it represents, I don't want to keep it."

"Let me show it to Thomas," Jenny said. "I imagine he would be interested in seeing it. Might inspire him to preach a sermon on the devil."

"I could stand one on the world, the flesh and the devil, the way I've been acting and feeling recently," Jed said as he pushed his chair back from the table. "Good lunch, Jenny." He patted her cheek as he went out onto the screened in porch to stretch out and relax before returning to his work.

When 8 o'clock came, Jenny was exhausted from all the work she had done in the August heat. She had taken a shower and slipped into a thin cotton dress. She stood infront of her mirror and combed her short red hair. Looking at her tanned face, she thought out loud, "My, am I looking old. I must get some creams and start working on my skin. I guess Vera will be all dressed up in one of her sheik summer pants outfits. This print cotton is me." She smoothed it down over her hips. "I'm gettin' a little plump too. *As* hard as I work, I don't know why I gain weight."

"Mom, that's because you're the best cook in the county." JoAnna said as she came into her mother's bedroom. She gently put her arm around her mother's shoulder. "But I like you just as you are. What's going on at Cybele's tonight?"

"I don't know," Jenny replied. "Vera just said she had somethin' to show her. Want to came along?"

"No, I think I'll just stay here and sit on the porch and talk to Jason. Won't be long until we each will be going our separate ways to college. Maybe Junie and Sam will come over like they used to on summer evenings. Remember how the four of us used to play until it was dark? I forgot, Sam won't be coming. He has already gone to the university for football practice. Wonder how he is doing. That is one young man that has a lot to learn about getting along with people. Junie is so different. He's always been so gentle and quiet."

"There's Vera now," Jenny said, grabbing her purse and going out the door. "Don't know how late I'll be."

Vera drove her air-conditioned Cadillac into Cybele's driveway. They were greeted by loud barks and growls. The Doberman ran back and forth across the front porch.

"I'm not budging one inch from this car until Cybele calls that dog," Jenny said firmly.

"Neither am I," Vera replied, pressing her hand on the car horn. "I do not understand why anyone, especially a preacher would want to keep such a vicious animal."

"They think he is gentle as a kitten. If he doesn't stay away from Bud Smith's chickens, there'll be no more dog," Jenny said.

"Calm down, Czar," Cybele scolded in a gentle but firm voice. The dog took one last look at the two women and ran away toward the graveyard behind the church.

"Is it safe," Vera called.

"Sure," Cybele replied. "He won't hurt you."

Vera and Jenny exchanged glances as they got out of the car.

They walked into Cybele's living room. She had the drapes pulled and the room appeared dark and gloomy.

"My! It's nice and cool in here," Vera said as she sat down on the couch. "What's all this?" She indicated the papers strown on the coffee table.

"These are my astrological charts," Cybele replied.

"I didn't know you were interested in astrology!" Jenny said with surprise.

"It's sort of a hobby," Cybele said. "My grandmother and aunt taught me how to use them. In fact they belonged to them. Also this old ouija board." She pulled the worn board from under the charts.

"I haven't seen one of those since I was a kid," Vera drawled.

"I remember getting one for Christmas from one of my cousins. After the holidays were over, my father, the late Judge Caldwell threw it into the fireplace and burned it up. He said it was of the devil and wouldn't let me play with it." She laughed, remembering her childhood.

"I always wanted to play with one," Jenny said, touching the faded letters and pictures. "Let's ask it somethin'."

Vera and Jenny, like two girls of ten, giggled as they placed the tips of their fingers on the pointer.

"What shall we ask it?" Vera giggled.

"Let's ask who will be your next husband," Jenny said teasingly.

"That's a good idea. Would be nice to know," Vera laughed.

"Perhaps, I'd better put that away," Cybele said. She reached out to take the board away. "It's very old, and I only keep it because it's been in my family for so long."

"And just when we were goin' to have some fun," Jenny complained.

Cybele disappeared into another room. When she returned, she was wearing a long flowing brightly colored caftan. Lifting her arms in the wide sleeves and twirling around, she said, "How do you like my lounging gown?"

"It's lovely!" Vera exclaimed.

"Wherever did you get it?" Jenny asked.

"The other day I was rummaging around in the attic and found a whole box of things. At first, I just thought it was junk, but I found this caftan and some other articles of clothing."

"Must have belonged to Mrs. Jones," Jenny said. "It's not really the type of thing that I could imagine her wearin'. It is pretty and very becomin' to you."

"Cybele, why did you ask me to come over tonight?" Vera asked.

Cybele suddenly appeared nervous. She shifted in her chair and cleared her throat. "Well, (addressing Vera) do you remember what we were talking about the night of the storm?"

"Yes!" Vera answered excitedly. "You mean we could try it tonight? Right here?"

"Try what? What are you two talkin' about?" Jenny asked.

"Jenny," Vera said, "I've been aiming to tell you something, but just haven't had the chance. It's about Cybele, er—you tell her Cybele."

"Not much to tell," Cybele said shyly. "I have special powers, not just everyone has them."

"What kind of powers?" Jenny asked. "The only power I know about is God's power."

"This is something that's been passed on to me by my ancestors," Cybele said.

"Let's get on with it," Vera said impatiently.

"Get on with what?" Jenny asked.

"Did you bring anything that belonged to Mr. Gray?" Cybele asked.

"I always carry his gold watch in my purse." Rummaging in her purse, she came out with a beautiful watch attached to a gold chain.

"Give it to me," Cybele said.

"What are you goin' to do?" wide eyed Jenny asked.

"Let's go sit around the dining table," Cybele said.

They followed Cybele into the dark kitchen.

"Aren't you goin' to turn on the light?" Jenny asked.

"No, darkness is better," Cybele said.

"I still don't know what we are goin' to do," Jenny said, fumbling in the dark to sit down on a chair at the table.

"We—rather Cybele is going to talk to my dead husband," Vera said in a loud whisper.

"Talk to the dead!" Jenny gasped.

"Let's be very quiet," Cybele said. "We must concentrate on the serious nature of what we are undertaking. I'm placing Mr. Gray's watch in the center of the table. Since I never knew him, I'll keep my hand on the watch. The two of you place your fingertips lightly on top of the table and touch the tip of each others middle fingers and meditate on the very last time you saw Mr. Gray alive. I'll repeat mentally, I will be the channel through whom the spirit of Mr. Gray will speak. I must do my best to make his spirit welcome."

The three women sat silently in the darkness. Suddenly a flash of lights beamed through the open front door as a car came into the driveway.

"Oh! That will be Thomas," Cybele said, breaking the silence. She flipped on the overhead kitchen light as Vera and Jenny blinked their eyes. "Please don't say anything to Thomas about what we've been doing," she said quickly.

"I think it's time we were goin' home," Vera said, gathering her purse. "We'll try this again some other time."

Vera and Jenny went out the door as Thomas came up the steps.

"No need for you ladies to rush off just because I came home," Thomas said.

"We better get along home, good night," Jenny echoed.

She and Vera got into the car and quickly drove away. They neither spoke for a few minutes.

"Well, I never!" Jenny exclaimed.

"You never what?" Vera asked.

"I never saw or heard of anything like this evenin'," Jenny declared.

"Jenny, let's don't tell anyone about this. I'm afraid we'll get Cybele into trouble."

"Don't worry. I have a lot of ponderin' over this before I could talk to anyone, even Jed."

They sat silently the remainder of the way to Jenny's house.

CHAPTER 12

THE FOLLOWING SUNDAY, the Bentleys attended church as usual. Vera Gray was not there. She had called Jenny on Thursday and told her she was going to Virginia to attend the wedding of a cousin on her father's side of the family.

Thomas Wilson removed his coat when he entered the pulpit and told all the men in the audience to do likewise. Wooden handled, paper fans with the picture of the Good Shepherd on one side and Hopkins Funeral Home on the other were swinging back and forth in the hands of every person in the audience. A hot breeze was coming through the open windows. Flies lazily found their way in, buzzing from person to person only to be shooed away by a paper fan.

Jenny was startled from her relaxed position that she had settled into after standing for the last hymn. Thomas was reading from the Old Testament. Jenny had turned in her Bible to the scripture he had announced as his text for his sermon. The words seemed to jump out at her from the page, and Thomas' deep voice was penetrating her very soul.

"There shall not be found among you anyone that maketh his son or his daughter to pass through the fire, or that useth divination, or a witch, or a charmer, or a consulter with familiar spirits, or a wizard or a necromancer. For all that do these things are an abomination unto the Lord; and because of these abominations the Lord thy God doth drive them out from before thee. Thou shalt be perfect with the Lord thy God. For these nations, which thou shalt possess, hearkened unto observers of times, and unto diviners, but as for thee, the Lord thy God hath not suffered thee so to do." Thomas closed the big pulpit Bible and said,

"May the Lord add His blessing to the reading of His Holy Word. Let us pray."

The fans stopped and a quiet hush came over the audience as everyone shifted in their seat, bowed their heads and closed their eyes.

"Our dear Heavenly Father," Thomas began in a strong voice. "Thank you for your word that is sharper than a two-edged sword. Hide me behind the cross of Jesus Christ and give me the words to say to those gathered here."

As he prayed, Jenny stole a quick look at Cybele sitting across the aisle. Cybele, dressed in her polyester blue dress her long hair falling about her shoulders, was gazing out the open window.

"I don't believe she has heard one word that Thomas has read from the Bible," Jenny thought, closing her eyes again and trying to concentrate on the prayer he was offering.

As soon as Thomas said amen, he started right into his sermon. His receding forehead broke out in giant drops of perspiration. He mopped them away with a slightly used handkerchief.

Jenny sat up straight and hung on every word.

"The Scripture I have chosen today is relevant to the time in which we are living. God was telling the children of Israel in the book of Deuteronomy that they should have nothing to do with the occult. This was true then, and it is true today. Anyone who is a believer in the Lord Jesus Christ as their Savior must have nothing to do with black magic, or call on the evil spirits for aid or be a fortune teller or ask a fortune teller for information. He or she should not be a serpent charmer, a medium or wizard or call forth the spirits of the dead."

Jenny wanted so badly to look toward Cybele, but she kept her eyes fixed on Thomas. She thought of Vera, and secretly wished she were here.

Thomas continued to warn his congregation against the Satanic influences that are at work in the world. He mentioned how much of this he had observed among the young people that he had worked with before coming to Langford. "Witch covens are prevalent on our university campuses," he said. "The Satanic church of America is well established in many of our cities. What are we doing about it?" Thomas stopped a second to wipe his brow.

Jenny took this opportunity to shift in her seat and look toward Cybele. Cybele was looking directly at Thomas as if she were taking in every word.

Thomas told of instances where he had first hand information on demon possession. He brought in New Testament scriptures about Christ casting out demons and ended his thirty minute sermon with Ephesians 6:12–13. "For we wrestle not against flesh and blood, but against the rulers of the darkness of this world, against spiritual wickedness in high places. Wherefore take unto you the whole armor of God, that ye may be able to withstand in the evil day, and having done all, to stand."

The people filed out of the church, shaking hands with Thomas and giving him words of encouragement and thanks for the timely message.

Jenny managed to slip by him without a word. She looked for Cybele, but it seemed she had disappeared.

Jed, Jenny, JoAnna and Jason got into the car. Everyone talked at once with the exception of Jenny about the exciting sermon that Thomas had preached.

As they arrived home, Jason said, "Mom, you're mighty quiet. Didn't you like the sermon?"

"I guess it just scared me," Jenny replied as she went into the kitchen to prepare lunch.

CHAPTER 13

JENNY EXCUSED HERSELF from the Sunday evening church service. She had a headache. After taking two aspirins, she stretched out across her bed. A light breeze was blowing through the open window. The big house was empty and quiet.

"This is the way it will be in a couple of weeks when JoAnna and Jason go away to college," she said out loud.

Her thoughts wandered back to Thomas' morning sermon. Was he speaking directly to me? Did he know what had taken place in his own house with his wife last week? Why wasn't Vera Gray at church this morning? She needed to hear that sermon as much as I did! What kind of person is Cybele? She just isn't like the rest of us. I still don't know what she was plannin' to do the other night. Why has it bothered me so much? Especially since this mornin'. Lord, I must talk to you about this.

She slipped off the bed and onto her knees. She rested her elbows on the bed, bowed her head and closed her eyes.

She spoke in an audible whisper, "Dear Lord, I don't quite understand what I've done wrong—no, Lord I do understand and I am convicted that even the mere thought of my substitutin' anythin' for Thee is a sin. Lord Jesus, forgive me for even thinkin' about talkin' to Vera's dead husband. I know that sort of thing is not for one of your children. I praise Thee and thank Thee that I am one of yours. Lord, I pray that you keep me in your care and give me the wisdom to say the right things to Cybele and Vera. Please don't let my family find out what I've done. I'm so ashamed."

Wet tears began to dampen her cheeks. "Dear Jesus, I feel better already, now that I've confessed my sin. Allow thy Holy Spirit to work in me, to guide and strengthen me, amen." She got back on the bed and immediately fell asleep. She was awakened when her family came in from church.

"Hey, mom," Jason called, "you should have been with us tonight. Thomas gave us some more of what he was talking about this morning. Before the service was over, he had me up in the pulpit with him, telling about some of the witch doctors and idol worship I saw in South America."

"You feelin' better, hon?" Jed asked. "You and Cybele must have the same disease. She wasn't at the service and Thomas said she had a headache."

"She's always having a headache," JoAnna said. "That girl is a weird one!"

"Was Vera Gray there?" Jenny asked.

"No," Jed replied. "I don't recall seein' her."

"She was goin' to Virginia for the weekend; guess she hasn't gotten back yet," Jenny said.

"Single woman, like her, with plenty of money can go most any place at anytime," Jed mused. "One of these days some poor man will marry her and help her spend that money that Mr. Gray left her."

"Let's all have some ice cream," JoAnna said, starting for the kitchen.

"Why don't we eat it on the porch," Jason replied.

Jenny kept wondering when she would have an oportunity to talk with Cybele. As she went about her work, she silently prayed that somehow she would be allowed to talk with her.

On Tuesday evening, Thomas telephoned Jed. "Could you go with me to the County Hospital? Stanley Holmes, (one of the church members) has been seriously injured in an automobile accident and isn't expected to live."

"I'll be ready in about ten minutes," Jed replied.

"I'll pick you up," Thomas said.

Jenny overheard the conversation. "Lord, this must be the time you want me to see Cybele alone," she thought.

"Think I'll go visit Cybele while you all are gone," Jenny told Jed.

"It will be a while before I can go as I have a cooker full of beans that I must take off the stove."

"Jenny, you're the most industrious wife any man ever had," Jed said, placing a kiss on her cheek.

"The Lord allows us to raise all these good vegetables, so it's up to me to preserve them."

JoAnna was out riding Duke. Jason had a date with a new girl who had recently moved to Langdon.

It was almost dark before Jenny was ready to go to Cybele's. She hurriedly wrote a note to JoAnna to tell her where she had gone. She decided it best not to call Cybele and tell her she was coming.

When Jenny arrived at Cybele's house, she noticed Vera Gray's Cadillac parked in the driveway.

"Wonder what they are up to," Jenny said to herself. "This will be a good time to talk to both of them."

The house was dark. Jenny cautiously walked up to the front door. She never quite trusted Czar, but he was nowhere in sight. The front door was closed. She rang the doorbell. Cybele came to the door. She was dressed in the long flowing caftan that she had worn the week before.

"Jenny, came in," Cybele said in a high pitched voice that was teeming with excitement." I'm so glad you are here."

Jenny followed Cybele through the dark living room and into the kitchen. A single black candle was burning in the center of the dining table. It took Jenny's eyes a moment to focus in the dimly lit room. Seated at the table was Vera and Aunt Tempie.

"Well, what is goin' on?" Jenny asked. "Aunt Tempie, what are you doin' here?"

The wrinkled black face turned to Jenny. The dark eyes rolled and her only reply was a cold stare that made a shiver run up Jenny's spine.

"Shuh!" said Vera in a whisper. "Don't interrupt, we're about to reach my dead husband."

Cybele pushed Jenny into a chair beside Aunt Tempie.

"Let us continue," Cybele said. "Concentrate, concentrate—Oh! Spirit of Mr. Gray speak to us."

Jenny jumped to her feet. "This is enough of this nonsense," she said in a forceful voice. She reached the wall switch and flooded the room with light. "I'm ashamed of you all!" Short little Jenny stood straight and tall. "Especially you, Cybele, after that sermon your husband preached on Sunday. You must not have heard one word he said. He used Scripture after Scripture to tell us that such as this is of Satan and we as Christians should have nothin' to do with it." She turned to Vera. "Vera Gray, you are as guilty as I am. We both know better than to have anythin' to do with talkin' to the dead. And you, Aunt Tempie, I've always known that you messed around with herb medicines, but I never thought you'd ever go so far as to try to talk to dead people."

"Jenny, calm down," Vera said. "I know in my heart that things like this are wrong, but I guess I just got carried away. What's the matter with Cybele? Look, she is on the floor. Has she fainted?"

The two women rushed over to her.

"Stay back," Aunt Tempie warned. "Stay away from her."

"She must be sick," Jenny said. "Look, she is frothin' at the mouth. Maybe she is havin' an epileptic fit. We ought to do somethin' instead of just standin' here. What's that she is mumblin'?"

"I'll call the rescue squad," Vera said.

"No," Aunt Tempie said, jumping between them and Cybele. "Don't nobody touch 'er. She is possessed. She is possessed with a demon." The wrinkled old face with the toothless mouth suddenly showed an expression that neither Jenny or Vera had ever seen before. "Don't even look at 'er. It's too dangerous."

The back screen door opened and the big Doberman Pincher bounded in. He stopped when he saw his mistress lying on the floor. He placed his big front paws just above her shoulders, and his hind paws on either side of her hips. He looked down into her face and began licking her forehead. A low growl came from his throat."

Jenny and Vera stood trembling, transfixed, afraid to move.

Suddenly the kitchen was filled with people. Jed's strong arms were around Jenny, holding her up. Junie Wade was holding onto Aunt Tempie and JoAnna had her arm around Vera's waist.

Thomas pushed the dog aside and got down on his knees beside his wife.

"Don't touch 'er," Aunt Tempie warned. "None of ya' understan'. She's possessed! I knowed hit from the fust time I ever seen 'er." Her dark eyes rolled from side to side. "She'll never fin' no peace on this earth until that ol' demon is cast out of 'er."

Thomas looked at Aunt Tempie. "You recognized her as being demon possessed?"

"I shore did."

"I have been suspecting this, but guess I just didn't want to recognize it in my own wife. Oh, my precious Cybele, what have I allowed to let happen to you?"

Aunt Tempie looked at him sympathetically, "Preacher, yo' aint't 'lowed nothin' to happen to 'er. She was born to this. Po' little ol' thin'." She shook her head.

"Then we'll just have to cast out that demon," Thomas declared.

Can you cast out a demon?" Jed asked in a quavering voice.

"I can't. But our Lord Jesus Christ can," Thomas replied. "Let us bow our heads and, each one pray as hard as we know how." In a loud voice he spoke slowly, "Lord Jesus Christ, we know you are all powerful. You have power over everything in Heaven and on earth. I beg you now to hear our plea for Cybele. In the name of Jesus Christ, I command this demon to come out of Cybele and to leave her alone forever."

Great drops of sweat fell from Thomas' forehead. It trickled down his face and splashed onto the floor beside Cybele. The room was very quiet. Cybele's body began to writhe as if every muscle was in great pain. A shrill sound of laughter came from deep in Cybele's throat. The sharp sound pierced the air. She thrashed from side to side. She struggled to sit up. She heaved and vomited down the front of the beautiful silk caftan.

The dog, standing near his master and mistress lunged forward through the crowd of people almost upsetting Aunt Tempie. The front screen slammed and a loud howl split the hot still August night.

"Th' ol' demon musta' went into the dog," Aunt Tempie muttered under her breath.

"Can that happen?" Jed asked.

"Demons went into the herd of swine in the Bible," Thomas replied hastily as he helped Cybele into a chair.

"Aunt Tempie, are you possessed too?" Junie asked.

"No chil'," Aunt Tempie replied slowly. "I'se the seventh daughter of a seventh daughter, an' wuz alwase told as a chil' that I'd has speshul powers. My mamie learned me sartin' things 'bout herb medicines an' potions. I'se knowed all kinds of things that my people before me used. You young folks depend on the doctors an' drug stores, but when I was cumin' long we'un never had sich as 'at. We'uns had to do th' bes' we knowed how."

Vera Gray began to cry. "Lord Jesus," she sobbed, "forgive me for my sin."

"I think we should all clear out and leave Thomas and Cybele alone," Jed said.

Cybele looked up at the mention of her name. In a feeble voice she said, "Please, don't call me Cybele anymore. That is the name the demon gave me. My real name is Ruth—after my mother." She began to cry.

Jenny's heart was touched by the pitiful pale form. "Thomas, I think Cyb—I mean Ruth needs to go to bed. She looks so tired. We'll all go along now."

JoAnna offered to drive Vera hone. Vera was in such a state, she agreed. Jed drove Jenny, Junie and Aunt Tempie home.

"Wonder whar that crazy ol' dog 'as gone," Aunt Tempie said as they rode along. "I never has liked 'em an' I'se more sceered ifen' the ol' devil is in 'em."

"This has been one strange evenin'," Jenny stated.

CHAPTER 14

WHILE THE MEN were still at the barn doing the morning milking, the county sheriff knocked on Jenny's kitchen door.

"Good mornin', Miz Jenny," Sheriff Godwin said, tipping his hat as Jenny opened the door.

"What can we do for you Sheriff?" Jenny asked. "How about a cup of coffee?"

"No thanks, I was wonderin' if Jed is around."

"He's still at the milkin' barn," Jenny replied. "Is somethin' wrong?"

"Maybe you can tell me. Does that new preacher at ya'lls church own a big black Doberman Pincher?"

"Yes, he does. What about it?"

"Bud Smith says it's been after his chickens. Last night it came in his yard a raisin' cain with his chickens and he got out his shot gun and blasted away. Killed that dog dead!" He shook his head and spit brown tobacco juice on the ground. "Too bad, that was one beautiful dog."

"Is that so?" Jenny asked, surpressing a smile. "I tell you Sheriff, I usually like dogs, but that was one I couldn't tolerate. It always acted like it was possessed—er—possessed by the devil. One minute it would be gentle and the next just tearin' about like somethin' crazy."

"Thought I'd stop by and tell you before I went over to the preacher's."

"Thanks, Sheriff," Jenny said. "I imagine they will want to bury it. They loved that old dog as much as we love our children.

"Good day, Mam," he said.

Later in the day, Thomas called to say that he and Ruth were going to Lake Stephen for a few days. Ruth was tired and wanted to get away. They would be back home in time for Sunday's services at the church.

Jenny managed to express sorrow over the loss of their dog.

Thomas had gone over to get the dog and had buried him without Ruth seeing him.

The week passed quickly. Jenny and JoAnna were shopping and sewing clothes for college. Jason was packing for his return to the University.

On Sunday morning the fields of the Bentley dairy farm were covered with fog. As Jed went out to milk, he called back to Jenny, "Look at all this fog. Remember what the old folks always say, 'as many snows in the winter as there are fogs in August. I think we'll have a lot of snow this winter."

"Would be a welcome relief after this hot summer," Jenny replied.

Ruth slipped into the seat beside Jenny at the preaching service. Jenny could hardly believe her eyes.

"Cybele, I mean Ruth, what have you done to your beautiful long hair?"

Ruth smiled, "I had it cut. How do you like it."

"Let me look at you. I like it. You look different. More grown up. I like your new dress."

"Thank you. I feel more grown up. In fact, I feel like a new person. I am a new person."

Before Thomas began his sermon, he asked Ruth to come to the podium with him.

He looked at her with loving eyes. "My wife has something to share with all of you. I know this is a little unusual, but it is something we feel we have to do."

He sat down and Ruth began to speak in a timid voice. "My name is Ruth Phillips Wilson." A gasp went over the audience. "I know most of you have thought of me as Cybele. My mother named me Ruth. She said it was a good Biblical name, the same name her mother gave her. My father was a showman with the circus and was gone more than he was at home. Once, when I was twelve years old, I went with him. That was my first time to meet my grandmother and my aunt. They were what you would call "gypsies." They worked fairs and carnivals as fortune tellers. I was fascinated by their ouija boards, tarot cards, crystal balls and astrological charts. My grandmother had a crystal ball that had been brought over from Europe by her ancestors. They showed me how to use these tools of the occult. And that is just what they are. I didn't know it then, but I know now that I opened myself up for demon possession." The audience looked startled. "My mother was a Christian and when I told her what I had learned, she forbid my ever speaking of it or seeing my father's people again. This made it even more intriguing to me. I secretly kept in touch with my aunt and grandmother. I had a talent for art and won a scholarship to college. This was my opportunity to get away from home and from my mother. Like many other young folks, I put aside my good home training and went the way of the world. I became part of the most evil of evils. I was taken into a witch coven. Yes, I worshipped Satan. My name was changed from Ruth to Cybele. Cybele means the Mother of the gods. The witch coven was discovered by the administration of the college and we were run out of town. We were scattered and somehow I got to California. My life had no purpose, no meaning. I had no desire to return to my parents. I tried to contact my grandmother and aunt, but discovered they had been killed in a fire. I spoke with a lady where they had been living and she said there was a package for me. I asked her to mail it. When I opened it, I discovered it contained their tarot cards, Ouija board and other tools of their trade."

"I continued to live in California. I'd paint a picture and sell it and buy another canvas and paint another. I lived in a commune and I didn't need many material things. After I left college, I did not worship Satan any more, but I did not worship God either. I was in limbo. I was possessed with a demon that made me do things I really didn't want to do. I would shoplift, I would lie, but I won't go into those things.

This demon would not let me alone. Sometimes it would go into our dog and make him do strange things. I would be so relieved, and every time I would think, now I am free, but then it would come back into me."

"When I met Thomas, I thought this is my chance to rid myself of the demon. He was so kind and I knew he had something I didn't have. As he has already told you, we were married after a very short courtship. It was last Monday night that the demon was cast out of me. I can truthfully say that now I am a child of God. I asked the Lord Jesus Christ to come into my heart and to cleanse me from all unrighteousness. I am a new creation. I truly have peace of mind. You might be interested to know that I called my mother and she was so happy to hear from me. She was especially happy that I had accepted Christ. She had continued to pray for me all these years. My father died last year." Tears began to well up in her eyes and she stepped from the platform and sat down beside Jenny.

Jenny put a loving arm around Ruth's shoulder.

Thomas preached a sermon that left his audience spell bound. His last words were: "Fellow Christians, the Lord has laid on our hearts that we should resign from our present position as your pastor and to return to California. My wife and I plan to go back to the area where we met and to preach Christ to the unsaved there. We will never forget you and we truly appreciate all you have done for us here in this beautiful church."

A strange quietness fell over the congregation. Some of the men got out handkerchiefs and blew their noses. Ladies wiped their eyes. The paper fans fluttered. The song leader arose and asked everyone to turn to page 78. The strains of "Abide With Me Fast Falls the Even Tide" floated out the windows and across the pastures and hills of the countryside.

CHAPTER 15

JENNY SAT ON the wide front porch with her mending. Quincy the cat stretched lazily at her feet.

"Just three months ago Thomas and Cybele, I mean Ruth, came into our lives. Now they are gone. They just drove away pulling a U-Haul-It trailer. JoAnna and Jason have gone away to college. Quincy, you're all I have to keep me company while Jed is out workin'... Thank you Lord for all my blessings."

www.ingramcontent.com/pod-product-compliance
Lightning Source LLC
Chambersburg PA
CBHW020800130626
46554CB00006B/2276